THE
CONSERVATION
EASEMENT
IN CALIFORNIA

THE CONSERVATION EASEMENT IN CALIFORNIA

by Thomas S. Barrett
& Putnam Livermore
for The Trust for Public Land

Island Press   Covelo, California

Library of Congress Cataloging in Publication Data

Barrett, Thomas S., 1947–
    The conservation easement in California.

    Bibliography: p.
    Includes index.
    1. Servitudes—California.   2. Land use—Law and legislation—California.   3. Natural resources—Law and legislation—California.   I. Livermore, Putnam, 1922–   II. Trust for Public Land (U.S.)   III. Title.
KFC163.5.B37   1983   346.79404'35   83–4329
ISBN 0–933280–20–3   347.9406435
ISBN 0–933280–19–X (pbk.)

Text and cover designer: Judith Barrett
Editor and production coordinator: Linda Gunnarson
Proofreaders: Carey Charlesworth and Netty Kahan
Typesetters: Dharma Press (text), Ad Comp and Solotype
         (titles and cover type), all of Oakland, California
Printer and binder: BookCrafters, Chelsea, Michigan

CONTENTS

FOREWORD   xi

ACKNOWLEDGMENTS   xiii

INTRODUCTION   1

CHAPTER ONE
CONSERVATION EASEMENT LEGISLATION
IN CALIFORNIA   9

LEGISLATIVE HISTORY   9

SUMMARY OF THE KEY LEGISLATION   20

Open-Space Easement Act of 1974 (Gov't Code
§§ 51070–51097)   21

California Conservation Easements Act of 1979
(Civ. Code §§ 815–816)   27

Scenic Easement Deed Act of 1959 (Gov't Code
§§ 6950–6954)   34

Land Conservation Act of 1965—Williamson Act
(Gov't Code §§ 51200–51295)   34

RELATED LEGISLATION   36

Article XIII, Section 8 (Formerly Article XXVIII) of the
California Constitution   36

1970 Amendments to the Planning and Zoning Law:
Open Space Land (Gov't Code §§ 65560–65570) and
Open Space Zoning (Gov't Code §§ 65910–65912)   37

California Timberland Productivity Act of
1982 (Formerly Z'berg-Warren-Keene-Collier
Forest Taxation Reform Act of 1976) (Gov't Code
§§ 51100–51155)   38

Open Space Subventions, 1972 (Gov't Code
§§ 16140–16154)   38

Open Space Amendments to Regional Park Districts
Law, 1975 and 1982 (Pub. Res. Code §§ 5500–5595);
Recreation and Park Districts (Pub. Res. Code
§§ 5780–5791)   39

Roberti-Z'berg Urban Open Space and Recreation
Program Act, 1976 (Pub. Res. Code §§ 5620–5632)   39

Open Space Maintenance Act, 1965 (Gov't Code
§§ 50575–50628)   40

Absolute Immunity of Public Land Trusts from Personal
Injury Liability on State-sanctioned Public Access
Lands; Qualified Immunity for Recreation on Private
Lands (Gov't Code § 831.5 and Civ. Code § 846)   40

Presumptions Affecting the Burden of Proof in Eminent
Domain Proceedings (Code of Civ. Proc. §§ 1240.670,
1240.680 and 1240.690)   42

State Coastal Conservancy (Pub. Res. Code §§ 31000–
31405); Santa Monica Mountains Conservancy (Pub. Res.
Code §§ 33000–33216)   42

Keene-Nejedly California Wetlands Preservation Act,
1976 (Pub. Res. Code §§ 5810–5818)   44

CHAPTER TWO
TAX INCENTIVES FOR THE DONATION
OF CONSERVATION EASEMENTS   45

FEDERAL TAX LAW   45

Background of the Federal Income Tax Deduction   45

The 1980 Federal Conservation Easement Income Tax
Deduction (I.R.C. §§ 170(f)(3)(B) and 170(h))   48

Public Benefit 51   Valuation 58   Perpetuity 60
Relation to the California Open-Space and
Conservation Easements Acts 63   Administrative
Matters 68   Wild and Scenic Rivers Act 69

Federal Estate and Gift Tax (I.R.C. §§ 2055(e)(2),
2106(a)(2)(e) and 2522(c)(2); § 2032A)   69

Capital Gains Tax   71

STATE TAX LAW 71

California Income Tax (Rev. & Tax. Code §§ 17214.2, 17214.7, 24357.2 and 24357.7) 71

California Inheritance Tax (Rev. & Tax. Code §§ 13957, 13841 and 13842); Open Space Land Dedication, 1978 (Gov't Code §§ 7301–7309) 71

California Property Tax 73

Open Space Property Tax Assessment (Rev. & Tax. Code §§ 421–430.5) 73   Related Property Tax Assessment Legislation 75   Assessment Valuation of Section 815 Conservation Easements 75 Impact of Proposition 13 77

Welfare Tax Exemption (Rev. & Tax. Code § 214); Special Provision for Open Space Lands (Rev. & Tax. Code § 214.02) 78

CHAPTER THREE
DRAFTING THE CONSERVATION
EASEMENT 81

CONSERVATION EASEMENT CHECKLIST 83

Parties 83

Legal and Qualitative Description of the Property 84

Type and Purpose of Easement 84

Statement of Intent of Grantor and Grantee 85

Reference to Documentation of Conservation Values To Be Preserved 85

Grant of Easement 86

Rights, Restrictions, Permitted Uses and Reservations 86

Allocation of Costs 91

Subsequent Deeds 92

Executory Limitation 92

Assignment   92

Integration   93

Severability   93

Costs of Enforcement   93

Habendum Clause   93

Date, Signatures and Acknowledgment   93

Exhibits   94

CHAPTER FOUR
CATALOG OF OTHER REAL PROPERTY
CONSERVATION TECHNIQUES   95

DEFEASIBLE FEE TECHNIQUES   95

FULL FEE TECHNIQUES   101

Purchase and Lease-back or Sell-back
Arrangement   102

Bargain Sale   103

Installment Sale   104

Sale or Gift of an Undivided Interest in Land   105

REMAINDER INTEREST   107

PURCHASE OPTION, RIGHT OF FIRST REFUSAL AND
COVENANT NOT TO SELL   107

LEASE   110

TRANSFER IN TRUST   111

COMMON LAW EASEMENT   113

RESTRICTIVE COVENANTS AND EQUITABLE
SERVITUDES   115

CONCLUSION   119

APPENDIX 1: LEGISLATION   121

Conservation Easements Act of 1979 (Civ. Code
§§ 815–816)   121

Open-Space Easement Act of 1974 (Gov't Code §§ 51070–51097)   123

Federal Tax Deduction: Tax Treatment Extension Act of 1980 (I.R.C. §§ 170(f)(3) and 170(h))   132

APPENDIX 2: SAMPLE CONSERVATION EASEMENT   135

NOTES   143

SELECTED BIBLIOGRAPHY   157

INDEX   165

FOREWORD

Pioneering new techniques of land protection for public enjoyment has been a goal of The Trust for Public Land since its founding. As we complete our tenth year, we can point with pride to the 45,000 acres of land that we have guided into public ownership for the access and enjoyment of the American public. At the same time, we recognize the value to the public of lands of great scenic appeal, as well as lands that harbor unique plant and animal habitats, and historic and archaeological sites. The public may never walk on these lands. In fact, their significant value might be destroyed by physical access. In their current use, however, they provide greenbelts around urban areas, foregrounds preserving aesthetic views of national and regional recreational attractions, and scenic farming and grazing countryside.

Public agencies and private land conservation organizations have turned to TPL for help in protecting these areas. Their aim has been to promote the continuation of the current use of these lands. Repeatedly, we have been asked to explain the concept of a conservation easement as a tool to use in accomplishing land protection goals.

Conservation easements are just beginning to see popular use in California. The National Park Service and the U.S. Fish and Wildlife and Forest services have long used easements in other parts of the country, but among public agencies in this state, only the California State Parks and Recreation Department has had much experience with easements, principally at Columbia State Historical Park in Tuolumne County. Local public agencies have been too unfamiliar with easements to make much use of them in their efforts to carry out their adopted general plans. In the private sector, conservation easements have been used extensively by land conservation organizations in the Northeast and mid-Atlantic states, but again very little locally. Of the few California examples, perhaps the most notable is The Nature Conservancy's conservation easement over Santa Cruz Island, off the Santa Barbara County coast.

Of benefit to government agencies and land trusts alike, California's enabling statutes for easements are among the most comprehensive anywhere. At the federal level, legislation enacted in 1980 made permanent the federal charitable tax deduction for gifts of conservation easements. Public agencies and land conservation organizations hailed this legislation for saving an important incentive for use of this valuable tool. As people become more familiar with it, the conservation easement should begin to see wide use in California.

The need for practitioners to know more about the conservation easement prompted Putnam Livermore, long-time California conservationist and attorney, to launch the substantial research project that *The Conservation Easement in California* represents. Thomas Barrett, an attorney with a National Park Service background, assumed principal responsibility for completing the research and writing the manuscript. The result of their collaboration is a superb handbook that, better than any other, can acquaint attorneys, landowners, public agency staffs, appraisers, tax counselors and land conservationists with the legal context for conservation easements in California.

The Trust for Public Land has welcomed the chance to sponsor this significant publication. As an organization known for its training and technical assistance to public agencies and local land trusts in real estate transactions, TPL more and more frequently is showing local communities how to use conservation easements along with fee acquisition and zoning techniques to protect significant natural and productive resources. This volume offers to us in the field the definitive resource that we have needed for some time. On behalf of The Trust for Public Land, I wish to thank Put Livermore and Tom Barrett for developing *The Conservation Easement in California*, and to express our appreciation to the Dean Witter Foundation for helping make its publication possible.

JENNIE GERARD
Director, Land Trust Program
The Trust for Public Land

ACKNOWLEDGMENTS

This book has been "in the works" for some time. Along the way, a number of people became involved whose contribution, invisible to the rest of the world, could not be more obvious to us now that we have the final product in hand. With gratitude we acknowledge the help of: Linda Johnson, who laid the groundwork for this project, doing considerable organizing, research and fact-finding in the crucial early stages; Kitty Codd, who prepared our working bibliography; Andrea Gilchrist, who, systematically reviewing and analyzing a large number of easement instruments, helped us bring at least a measure of coherence to our treatment of easement drafting; Judy Motoyama, who helped to coordinate it all; and Maureen Carroll, Lynne Azevedo, Paul Merar, David Goldberg, Mark Kapp and Mary Ellyn Gormley, who patiently and professionally worked draft after draft of the manuscript through their magical word processors. We are grateful to the many people who reviewed and commented on the manuscript at various stages of its development, including Martin Rosen, Ralph Benson and Jennie Gerard—President, General Counsel and Land Trust Program Director, respectively, of The Trust for Public Land—and especially Professor William T. Hutton of Hastings College of the Law, on whose expertise in the tax aspects of this field we leaned heavily. We thank Commissioner John F. Dunlap of the Workers' Compensation Appeals Board for taking the time to confirm the accuracy of our account of the history of the open space legislation he sponsored as a state assemblyman, and later state senator, from Napa. We thank our colleagues at Chickering & Gregory, several of whom read and offered constructive criticism of the manuscript, and all of whom remained supportive of the project through the countless hours it consumed. Finally, we are forever indebted to the late James Walton, for many years Land Manager, and later Vice President, of Leslie Salt Co., whose special sense of the importance of finding reasonable means of protecting one of the world's finest examples of open space, the San Francisco Bay, helped motivate us to write this book. We dedicate it now to his memory.

INTRODUCTION

Land is America's most valuable resource, and no state is richer in land than California. The majestic mountains, fertile valleys, deep coastal forests, and the great rivers, lakes and estuaries of California offer up a landscape of Biblical fullness; it is the promised land within the promised land, the culmination of American wealth and dreams, the Golden State.

Not surprisingly, California has grown in a short time to be the most populous of any state, and still it continues to grow. But even for so rich a place, the pace has been too swift. California's resources, bountiful as they are, are not limitless and have become subject to increasingly more competitive demands. Urban and agricultural users clamor for space and water, and it is clear that not all can be satisfied. Planning and control of resource use is imperative if the state's natural riches are to be fairly distributed among its people. Land is the key. The source. The health and wealth of Californians depend on how they use their land. The great farms, forests, grasses and fisheries are what sustain life here. To the extent these things are allowed to be depleted by growth, growth will be self-defeating, a prelude to disaster. To remain bountiful, the California landscape must be respected, so that it can continue to support Californians and their children as generously as it has until now.

The central importance of open land in the California dream is not well understood because many of the life-giving functions of land happen invisibly. There was a time when open space was looked upon only as a scenic amenity, an aesthetic luxury good for the mind and soul but little else. To set aside open space was to sacrifice what in economic terms was the "highest and best use" of the land in order to provide a modicum of psychological enjoyment. Although preservation of scenic beauty is still recognized as an important goal in land conservation, the benefits of open space are now understood to be far more diverse. With the increased awareness of the ecological interrelationship of all living things has come the realization that leaving land open serves many purposes essential to the well-being of

1

the human community. Cropland, forest land, grassland, wetland, flood plain, watershed, aquifer, river, lake: all directly contribute to the quality of our air, water and soil, the very elements of our survival. To protect these things is to assure that our life line remains intact. Despite the appearance of technological self-sufficiency, our dependence on the land is absolute. For the land to sustain us, every link in the ecological chain must be strong. The preservation of open space is a necessity, not a luxury.

The development of land for residential, commercial or other non-land-related use is, for all practical purposes, an irreversible commitment to such use. Once developed, land almost never reverts to open use, particularly land developed for residential purposes. Because there is an abundance of good land in California, it is not surprising that so much of it has been inefficiently used. Until recently, there has been little effort to match uses with the types of land most suited to them. Prime agricultural land adjacent to urban areas, for example, has been rapidly converted to low-density residential use because it is so easy to build on. Only within the last few years has it become apparent that this needless squandering of agricultural lands has drastically undercut the ability of potentially self-sustaining regions to remain supplied with fresh meat and produce at reasonable prices and has left them potentially vulnerable to critical shortages caused by national and international pressures on supply.[1] Other instances could be cited of unchanneled development leading to the depletion or deterioration of local water supplies, flooding and erosion. The message is a simple one. The careless use of our resource base can and should be avoided. Resource protection is not incompatible with growth, only indiscriminate growth. Lands should be put to their best use, and development should be channeled away from those lands whose best use can only be achieved if they are left open.

Standing in the way of sound land conservation practices in California and elsewhere in our country is the deeply embedded social and legal tradition that land ownership carries with it the right to use one's land in any way one wishes, short of creating a nuisance—a right that implies, most importantly, the right to maximize the profitability of one's land. In recent years, various legal techniques have been introduced in an effort to reconcile this tradition with the need to conserve open space. Most are variations on zoning, often with some form of compensation added to soften the regulatory effect. Planned unit developments, subdivision ordinances, cluster-site housing, phased annexation, mitigation, exaction, compensable regulation and transferable development rights: there are many approaches to the problem, some still quite experimental. Transferable development rights, for example, contemplate the creation of a market in which landowners whose lands are designated for protection can transfer the development potential of their land, foreclosed by regulation, to persons wishing to develop other land that has been zoned for development. The purchase of development rights would enable landowners in those areas zoned for development to build at higher, more profitable densities than otherwise would be permitted. Conceptually, the transferable development rights idea, based on the separability of the right to develop property from the property itself, is a departure from popular notions of property rights and, no doubt, will take some time to catch on. However, it represents a serious attempt to balance society's need for open space with the individual's right to fairness. Not yet widely used, it is a concept to which a number of communities are beginning to turn as the adverse social and environmental effects of uncontrolled development become more visible.

The transferable development rights technique builds on a fundamental legal theory of land ownership that conceives of real property not concretely, as land and improvements, but abstractly, as a bundle of rights. Far from being indivisible, real property can be seen, in the light of this theory, to be divisible in many ways: spatially or temporally, tangibly or intangibly. An owner of land owns not only what can be seen (what in legal terms might be called the surface rights) but also what cannot be seen (including air rights, mineral rights, access rights and the right to possess or develop any of these). The owner can hold all these rights himself or divest himself of any of them as he sees fit. He can create present interests in others (e.g., a mineral lease) or future interests (e.g., ownership commencing at his death, a remainder interest). This concept of property ownership has led to another approach to land conservation, similar in some ways to transferable development rights but more firmly rooted in the English-American legal tradition: the open space or conservation easement.

Easements draw on a long history of common law usage. An easement is an incorporeal but, for that, no less definite interest in real property entitling the easement owner to some limited use of the property of another or restricting the landowner's use of the property for the benefit of the easement owner. The type of easement most commonly encountered is a right of way, as for an access road or utility pipeline. However, the easement device can be adapted to serve a wide variety of needs, and, when adapted to conservation purposes, it provides a degree of economy, flexibility and specificity that makes it unique among conservation techniques.

Easements have been used for conservation purposes at various times and by various persons and governmental agencies throughout this century with little fanfare but to great effect. The technique is simple. A landowner grants an easement that limits by its terms his right to develop certain property. For its part, the grantee of the easement assumes the responsibility of assuring that the terms of the easement are honored. It is a transfer of development rights not for the purpose of using them elsewhere, but rather for the purpose of not using them at all.

Most of the early conservation easements were for scenic purposes. The federal government employed scenic easements to preserve the view along the Blue Ridge Parkway and the Natchez Trace Parkway in the 1930s and 1940s; Wisconsin did the same along the Great River Road and other state highways in the 1950s. In the 1960s, the National Park Service acquired scenic easements to protect integral views at Mount Vernon and several other Eastern historical parks. More recently, the Park Service has used scenic easements in the Sawtooth National Recreation Area in Idaho and has coupled scenic easements with access rights along federally designated wild and scenic rivers and on the Appalachian Trail.

The easement technique has been used historically to serve critical ecological needs as well. In by far the largest conservation easement program to date, the U.S. Fish and Wildlife Service has been using easements since the 1950s to preserve wild waterfowl breeding habitats in the glacier-created "pothole" wetlands of Minnesota and the Dakotas. To prevent farmers, for whom these wetlands represent only a waste of potential cropland, from burning, draining and filling them, the Fish and Wildlife Service has purchased perpetual easements prohibiting such activities over approximately 1,100,000 acres of wetland.[2] Whereas the outright purchase of so much acreage would have been prohibitively expensive, the easement approach, by focusing only on those few property rights that are essential to saving the crucial waterfowl habitat, has made it possible for the government to protect four times as much habitat as it could have otherwise.[3]

In addition to using easements in its own programs, the federal government has made funds available to state and local governments for the acquisition of scenic and open space easements under such diverse cooperative programs as Title III of the Highway Beautification Act of 1965[4] and the Open Space Land Program of the U.S. Department of Housing and Urban Development.[5]

There are other instances of the successful use of the conservation easement technique by public entities. In New York, Wisconsin and Minnesota, for example, state agencies have acquired fishing easements from owners of land adjacent to trout streams.[6] In California, the easement technique has been used since 1933 by the State Department of Parks and Recreation to restrict the use of lands in and adjacent to state parks. Although the authority exists to purchase or condemn easements, the Parks Department has acquired its easements primarily by gift, to the benefit of such parks as Point Lobos State Reserve, Pfeiffer–Big Sur State Park and Columbia State Historic Park.[7] California law also contemplates the acquisition of scenic easements along state and interstate highways.[8] In short, although the conservation easement is still widely perceived as something of a novelty, there is a substantial body of history to draw upon regarding its use.

Today, those most likely to call upon this history are not public agencies but private ones, such as local land trusts and local, regional or national conservation organizations. The reason for this is twofold. Fiscal constraints on governments have grown increasingly tighter in the last several years. Tax abatement measures, such as Proposition 13 in California, coupled with the inflated cost of essential and entitlement services, have made it harder for governments, particularly local governments, to take the lead in land conservation. Secondly, many private citizens are now alert to the damaging consequences of uncontrolled growth and are taking the initiative to protect their own communities from them. These are people with a sense of place and history, with ties to their land, who are willing to accept the responsibility of assuring the continuity of natural and historical values in their communities. They are learning about the various tools available to them to preserve these values and are beginning to use them.

In the New England and Atlantic states, local land trusts have been protecting vital local resources for many years, and some have been using easements for this purpose since the early 1960s.[9] More recently, in California, local citizens have established nonprofit land trusts in Humboldt, Sonoma, Monterey, Marin, Napa, San Mateo, Santa Barbara, Orange, Los Angeles, Santa Cruz, Mendocino, San Diego and Riverside counties to take on the job of preserving important land areas in their communities. In many cases the land these trusts seek to protect is of national as well as local significance. In response to this wakening interest in the local land trust idea in California, The Trust for Public Land, a national land conservation organization, has begun to extend training and technical assistance to these new organizations and to other interested people in an effort to create a cooperative network of land trusts throughout the Western states and the nation.

In the hands of the local land trusts the easement technique should become increasingly more refined as these groups apply it to the varied conservation needs of their communities. Some of what the local land trusts may want to do will involve them in scientific and legal complexities for which there is little precedent. However, the fact that they are local, community-based organizations working among their neighbors to protect local resource values in which they have a personal stake makes them right for the task.

This book was written for the private conservation movement, though no argument is made that open space preservation can or should be left exclusively to the private sector. To do so would be to abdicate the fundamental responsibility of government to plan and provide for the resources that will be needed to sustain the highest possible quality of life for present and future generations. But there is an important role to be played by private conservation organizations, particularly the local land trusts, and it is one that no governmental agency could possibly be as fit to play. Legislation, both state and federal, has been passed in recent years to give these private organizations the basic tools they will need. The utility of the conservation easement, potentially subject to attack as too novel for the law of easements to enforce, has been secured by legislative action in California and many other states. In addition, in California, the means have been made available for land trusts and other conservation organizations to act both within and without local governmental planning channels to bring the conservation easement technique to bear on conservation problems. Finally, both California and federal tax laws have been amended to create incentives for use of the conservation easement, giving conservation organizations the selling points they need to persuade landowners to participate.

If the optimum protection of open space is to be achieved, it must be through a combination of techniques and a mix of public and private sector involvement. However, the focus of this book is on the easement technique and its use by the private sector. Alternative techniques available to the private sector, as well as some related governmental measures for open space preservation, are discussed as a means of establishing the context for the conservation easement. Legal and historical background detail is provided for the same purpose. The real work of this book is to make the conservation easement accessible to conservation organizations, the new local land trusts and their attorneys. To that end, California state legislation governing conservation easements and the important state and federal tax implications of donating conservation easements are explored. In addition, the issues involved in drafting an easement (perhaps the most problematic aspect of the easement acquisition process) are outlined, and solutions to specific drafting problems are proposed.

The whole is intended as a general legal reference work for the people who will be making conservation easement law. It gives entry to the subject matter but makes no pretense of exhausting it. Tax strategy, for example, often crucial in the event, is hardly touched on here. In addition, no attempt is made to chronicle the experiences of those people who have already put the conservation easement to good use. The purpose of this book is to tell what the law is with respect to conservation easements in California. Individual experiences will pinpoint where specific problems are, but first the law must be known and understood for the lessons of experience to be meaningful. As experience with the conservation easement device grows, however, there can be little doubt that a handbook, with case studies, will follow.[10]

A final note. For the sake of clarity, the term *conservation easement* is used generically throughout this book to include all essentially similar restrictions on land use variously, and often interchangeably, denominated as "conservation easements," "conservation restrictions," "scenic easements," "open space easements" and "preservation easements." Occasionally, it is necessary to use some other term, to conform to the usage adopted by specific legislation. It is, for example, necessary to use the term *open space easement* when discussing the Open-Space Easement Act. However, unless the context indicates otherwise, the term *conservation easement*, as used here, should be understood to include all easements for a conservation purpose however designated in legislation or popular parlance.

CHAPTER ONE

CONSERVATION EASEMENT LEGISLATION IN CALIFORNIA

T o understand the conservation easement approach to land conservation problems it is helpful to have some acquaintance with the historical evolution of open space legislation in California. In addition, it is important to be familiar with the terms of the principal statutes dealing with conservation easements—the Open-Space Easement Act and the Conservation Easements Act—and to have a sense of the relationship of those statutes to other open space legislation. This chapter outlines the history of open space legislation in California, discusses the provisions of the Open-Space Easement Act and the Conservation Easements Act in some detail and briefly summarizes the Williamson Act, the Scenic Easement Deed Act and selected other statutes that have been included here because each of them has, in varying degrees, some connection to the core conservation easement legislation.

LEGISLATIVE HISTORY

The rapid transformation of California from a predominantly agrarian to a largely urban culture has created great pressure to develop its open space and agricultural lands, particularly those lands bordering directly on burgeoning urban centers. Under conditions of rapid urban growth, speculation in open lands prime for development sends their market value up, often astronomically. This increased value alone encourages the abandonment of open space and agrarian uses of land in favor of ready profits. Historically, however, even those persons who might otherwise have resisted the temptation to sell their lands for immediate gain were confronted by a still more compelling reason to sell out in the face of urban growth. Because the new speculative value of their lands usually resulted in higher tax assessments based on the highest and best use for the land (development), farmers and other owners of open space lands were subjected, in some locations, to a property tax burden that approached or even exceeded the income they were able to derive from the most diligent management of their lands. In such cases, continued farming or other open space uses were no longer rational alternatives and the landowners were forced to sell. In this way, market value assessment—the tradition in most states and a constitutional mandate in California—came to play a central if unwitting role in the ill-advised or premature conversion of open lands to urban uses.

The first tentative steps taken by the California legislature to protect open space were aimed at abating the adverse effect of property taxes on open space. In the 1950s, Santa Clara County—historically a prime agricultural region—experienced a growth explosion. During that time, municipalities throughout the county were vying with each other for additional territory and the increased tax base that would go with it. In 1955, in an attempt to shield at least some of the region's rich farmland from development, the legislature added Section 35009—the so-called greenbelt statute—to the Government Code.[11] The greenbelt statute, limited by its terms to Santa Clara County, did not address the problem represented by the application of market value assessment techniques to open space lands, but rather sought only to prevent forced annexation from adding to the property tax burden of farmers already beset by high assessments. Section 35009 permitted farmers to choose to have their lands zoned exclusively for agriculture. If a farmer did opt for agricultural zoning, a municipality would then be required to obtain his consent prior to annexing his land. In the first few years of the program, some 50,000 acres of prime farmland were brought under the protection of greenbelt zoning.[12]

Section 35009 was never more than stopgap legislation. The voluntary nature of the program, the uncertain duration of the restrictive zoning, the failure to address the more critical market value assessment problem and the fact that Section 35009 was confined by its terms to Santa Clara County: all testified to the tentative nature of this first legislative step. Nevertheless, attention was at least focused on the adverse impact of property taxation on farm and open space lands, and, in 1957, the legislature began to look at the market value assessment problem itself. In that year Section 402.5 was added to the Revenue and Taxation Code, providing that land zoned and used for agriculture or recreation was to be assessed only on the basis of factors relative to that use. While market value assessment was to remain the rule, assessors were not to look to those uses for which agricultural or recreational land was naturally adaptable regardless of current use—normally fair game for valuation and assessment—but only to the highest and best use legally available for the property as zoned at the time of assessment. The zoned use standard was to be applied in those cases where "no reasonable probability" existed—as judged by zoning trends in a given jurisdiction—that the land would be rezoned in the near future for a use that would increase its value.

In practice, this test proved impossible to meet. Assessors regularly discounted the effect of zoning on market value due to its notorious impermanence, and, in any event, Section 402.5 contained a fundamental flaw. Because legislative bodies cannot restrict the future exercise of their power, there could be no assurance that rezoning would not occur, hence no basis for a finding of "no reasonable probability" under Section 402.5.[13] To remove this flaw, Section 402.5 was amended in 1965 to create a rebuttable presumption that a zoning ordinance enacted pursuant to a general plan was permanent. This change shifted the burden of proving impermanence to the assessors; but, since there usually was ample evidence of the changeable nature of zoning, the burden was relatively easy to meet in most cases.[14] Section 402.5 proved a weak beginning for farmland and open space protection.

In 1959, changing course somewhat, the legislature took a tentative step aimed at more actively involving local governments in open space protection. In that year, as a response to the specific need expressed by landowners in Monterey County for a ready means to protect their coastline against the threat of impending development, the Scenic Easement Deed Act was passed.[15] Its purpose was to enable local governments to accept grants of "scenic easements" from landowners who wished to preserve special scenic and aesthetic values of their lands.[16] The Scenic Easement Deed Act was the first such piece of legislation in the United States.[17] For the first time, a legislature had recognized open space conservation as a valid public purpose, even in cases where no public access would be provided. For this reason especially, the Scenic Easement Deed Act represented a significant policy advance. However, the Act itself, as drafted, proved ineffectual.

In spite of the fact that the federal government and others had been using easements to preserve scenic landscapes since the early 1930s, the conservation easement concept was still not widely known in 1959, and the Scenic Easement Deed Act reflected this unfamiliarity. The Act was very brief. It authorized local governments to act to protect open space through the acquisition of scenic easements but provided no guidance on how to implement the authority given, outlined no planning function, established no fund for purchasing easements and extended no power of eminent domain. The Act contained no incentives to encourage participation and was silent with respect to the tax implications of an easement transfer. As experience with Section 402.5 of the Revenue and Taxation Code was demonstrating, assessors were slow to find that zoned developmental restrictions on land constituted permanent reductions in value worthy of lower assessed valuation. Without any direction from the legislature, assessors were no more likely to treat restrictions imposed by the novel scenic easement as permanent.[18] In the absence of certainty that the granting of scenic easements in which they gave up valuable development rights would relieve them of paying taxes based on those rights, landowners were understandably reluctant to make use of the Act.[19] In short, the Scenic Easement Deed Act, however important as a pioneering statement of public policy, was of no practical value by itself. It went unused.[20]

In 1962, taking yet another approach, the legislature flirted with the idea of a deferred tax program for relieving the property-tax-induced developmental pressures on agricultural lands. The idea was submitted to the electorate as Proposition 4 and was narrowly defeated. Proposition 4 would have allowed owners of farmland to defer as much of the tax on their property as was attributable to development potential until such time as they decided to sell their lands to developers. The government could then have recouped taxes for the seven years immediately preceding a sale.

Although superficially attractive, the deferred tax program had many inherent weaknesses that would have rendered it incapable of reducing speculation in farmlands close to urban areas or of preventing haphazard urban sprawl. The main flaw was that it required no long-term commitment to farming, with the result that it would have benefited both bona fide farmers and speculators indiscriminately.[21] In addition, under Proposition 4, the highest and best-use market value approach to real property assessment would have remained in place, albeit on a deferred basis. Although the legislature was groping for a way to moderate the adverse effect of the traditional market value approach to tax assessment, it remained, for the time being, too timid to attack that standard head on. The defeat of Proposition 4 undoubtedly hastened the day when it would have to do so.

In 1965, ten years after it began the search for a satisfactory method to channel development away from lands that were perceived to have a greater public value if left undeveloped, the legislature took another tack. Again the focus was on preserving agricultural lands, this time in the California Land Conservation Act of 1965, popularly known as the Williamson Act.[22] In its original form, the Williamson Act was yet another attempt at an end-run around the adverse effect of full market value assessment. The Act combined governmental planning with private choice by providing a contractual method for restricting the use of agricultural lands located in governmentally designated "agricultural preserve" zones. By the terms of the Act, farmers and local governments could contract to restrict property to agricultural uses for a minimum of ten years, with provision for an automatic extension of one year at each anniversary of the contract until either party gave notice of its intent not to renew, after which the contract would be allowed to expire at the end of the time remaining in the term. Under such a system, land under contract would be protected as agricultural open space for at least ten years and potentially in perpetuity. The intent of the legislature was to provide a means of restricting land use that was sufficiently fixed, certain and binding to cause the market value of lands subject to restriction to fall. With the fall in market value, the assessed value of the land likewise would be reduced, and tax relief for farmers would result.

To make the case for tax relief even more compelling, the legislature repealed Section 402.5 of the Revenue and Taxation Code, described earlier, and adopted Section 402.1 in its place. Section 402.1 mandated that any "enforceable restriction" on land of whatever type—zoned or contractual—would have to be considered by assessors in evaluating real property for tax purposes. The rebuttable presumption of Section 402.5—that restrictions pursuant to a general plan were permanent and therefore constituted "enforceable restrictions"—was carried over into Section 402.1. Companion legislation added Section 1630 to the Revenue and Taxation Code, establishing a procedure whereby a local government could give a letter of intent to a landowner, for evidentiary purposes, stating that it did not intend to terminate the restriction on his land.

With this legislation, the legislature came as close to equating the value of property to its legally permissible use as it could without seeking to amend the California Constitution to provide an alternative to market value assessment. It was not enough. The Williamson Act received little use during its first two years on the books.[23] The tax consequences of voluntary land restriction seemed too uncertain to most landowners. If open space and agricultural land preservation was to become a reality in California, assessors would have to be denied the full market value assessment technique in evaluating lands devoted to a protected purpose. Nothing short of that would be enough to encourage open space landowners and farmers to take the self-limiting step of restricting use of their lands. The financial risk was simply too great.

In 1966, the legislature finally went all the way. Article XXVIII,[24] to amend the California Constitution to permit the legislature to designate certain lands as eligible for tax valuation based on their actual use rather than their market value, was proposed to the electorate as Proposition 3, won ratification and became law. Although to this point, with the exception of the moribund Scenic Easement Deed Act of 1959, the central concern had been, for all practical purposes, with agricultural lands, Article XXVIII was broadly drafted, setting forth a policy of protection for open space lands generally, on aesthetic as well as economic grounds. Article XXVIII was to be the font of open space legislation in California. The people of the state had ratified the use of preferential tax treatment to conserve open space, and the legislature now had the power to back up any open space program it might choose to institute with the property tax incentives necessary to encourage its use. The terms of Article XXVIII gave the legislature full power to define open space, to specify what constituted an enforceable restriction on open space lands and to determine the formula for assessing enforceably restricted open space lands. As a result of this profound conceptual and practical liberation from market value assessment, the state legislature, not the local assessor, held the key to protection of agricultural and open space lands. What remained was for the legislature to determine how much of that power it wished to use and the way in which it should use it.

Immediately following the passage of Article XXVIII, the legislature appointed a Joint Committee on Open Space Land whose purpose was to study existing open space legislation and make recommendations to the full body on how best to augment that legislation in light of the new authority conferred by Article XXVIII. Interim legislation was passed to provide for immediate implementation of mandatory use-related valuation for open space protection devices already available under the Williamson Act and the Scenic Easement Deed Act. Under that legislation (codified at Sections 421–425 of the Revenue and Taxation Code), a Williamson Act contract was defined as an enforceable restriction qualifying property under contract for use valuation, regardless of the effect of the contract on the market value of the property. A scenic easement deed was likewise to be considered an enforceable restriction if its terms were determined to be substantially as restrictive as a Williamson Act contract.[25]

With the addition of Sections 421–425, the Williamson Act, although voluntary and therefore no guarantee of comprehensive preservation, became a serious agricultural land protection tool. By 1969, twenty-three counties had made use of the program, restricting more than two million acres of land to agricultural use.[26] It is estimated that at the present time more than sixteen million acres—16 percent of the state's land area and one-third of all privately held land in the state—are protected under Williamson Act contracts.[27]

Of course, the true measure of success of the Williamson Act or of any differential taxation program is whether it slows down the accelerating conversion of agricultural land to urban use. There is evidence that, because the lands enrolled in the program are predominantly remote from urban centers, the Williamson Act has done little to prevent development in those urban fringe areas most vulnerable to it.[28] In addition, the Act may do little more than temporarily delay the conversion of lands subject to its restrictions, affording some landowners the flexibility to time the conversion of their lands to achieve the maximum return.[29] Nevertheless, because of the sheer acreage involved, it must be said that the Williamson Act, while no panacea, has played the most significant role in conserving California open lands of any legislation to date. The Scenic Easement Deed Act, however, although finally put to use by three counties,[30] remained even after passage of Sections 421–425 a virtually untried novelty—too little understood to be really useful to the landowners and local governments for whose benefit it was intended. While the legislature would make certain improvements in the Williamson Act, by 1969 broad participation in the program had proven its usefulness. The task remained, however, for the legislature to devise some similarly effective method for protecting nonagricultural open space.

In 1969, on the recommendation of the Joint Committee on Open Space Land, the legislature expanded the potential coverage of the Williamson Act contract mechanism to include lands devoted to recreational and open space as well as agricultural uses. Certain wetlands, tidal areas, salt ponds, wildlife habitats and public outdoor recreation areas were made eligible for inclusion in agricultural preserves and Williamson Act contracts. In addition, restriction by contract of areas adjacent to officially designated state or county scenic highways was made mandatory upon the request of landowners. More significantly for our purposes, and again upon the Joint Committee's recommendation, the legislature also passed the Open-Space Easement Act of 1969.[31] The intention was to provide what was missing in the Scenic Easement Deed Act of 1959: a procedure for the acquisition of open space easements by local governments that was clear and specific and that was tied into the local general planning function. Under the Open-Space Easement Act, local governments were empowered to accept and enforce open space easements and to withhold building permits for the construction of any improvements that would violate such easements. An open space easement was to be, in effect, a transfer to the public of all development rights not expressly reserved by a landowner for a minimum term of twenty years. In return for the relinquishment of such rights, the landowner would be eligible for the same use-related assessment valuation that had been devised for lands under Williamson Act contracts. The scenic easement deed remained eligible for such treatment as well, but the Open-Space Easement Act was clearly designed to displace the earlier Scenic Easement Deed Act by force of its far greater specificity.

The Open-Space Easement Act of 1969 was an improvement over the 1959 Act, but, like its predecessor, it went virtually unused. By 1974, "only a minuscule amount of land" had been placed under open space or scenic easement restriction.[32] The Williamson Act was upstaging the open space legislation. As reported by the State Resources Agency, the Open-Space Easement Act was "greatly overshadowed by the Williamson Act which ha[d] been used in about 95% of all cases to obtain reduced taxes for open space purposes."[33]

Because there was a perceived need for an open space law complementary to the Williamson Act, one that allowed for the protection of open space outside the boundaries of agricultural preserves, the legislature tried again in 1974 to write an open space easement law that people would use. The Open-Space Easement Act of 1974[34] was the result. The 1974 Act was "designed to make the open space easement device more attractive to both local government and landowners as a method for preserving open space if a parcel of land does not qualify for the Williamson Act."[35] The basic framework of the 1969 Act was retained, but a number of liberalizing changes, informed by the Williamson Act model, were made. The most important change was the reduction in the minimum term of an easement from twenty to ten years. In addition, annual automatic renewal and the right of a landowner to petition for abandonment were added. It was hoped that these changes would lead to wider use of the open space easement and that greater protection for agricultural land and other open space would result.

In spite of the legislature's good intentions, the immediate fate of the 1974 Act was no different from that of the 1959 and 1969 Acts: it went unused.[36] In the absence of a statewide program for open space preservation, integrating open space planning with funding for the governmental purchase or condemnation of open space lands, the state and local governmental role in preserving open space remained, it would appear, too passive to be very effective. Few easements were granted to governmental entities because local governments either had no real interest in them or actually opposed them due to the expense and loss of property taxes involved.[37] This lack of enthusiasm on the part of local governments, coupled with a broad distrust of local government on the part of landowners, blocked any chance of success the easement legislation might otherwise have had.[38]

In 1977 an effort was made to correct the deficiencies in California's open space easement legislation by opening up the process to include nonprofit conservation organizations as eligible recipients of easements under the Open-Space Easement Act of 1974. In so doing, the state legislature hoped to enlist the energies of the private conservation movement, and specifically the newly emerging local land trusts, for the task of selling the open space easement idea to landowners. State Senator John F. Dunlap, author of both the 1974 Act and the 1977 amendments,[39] stated this purpose in a press release issued on April 14, 1977: "I am amending the Open-Space Easement Act to include non-profit organizations because I believe that private and public land trusts are capable of aggressively pursuing open space easements in a manner that governmental agencies are unable to do, and from sources previously untapped."

Local governments would continue to bear whatever costs might result from the loss of tax revenues due to the granting of open space easements, but other costs that may have inhibited local governmental participation in the open space easement program (the expense of surveys, title searches, appraisals, negotiations, inspections and any necessary litigation) could now be shifted to willing nonprofit conservation organizations. In an example of public and private sector interdependence, the government placed its best hope for the fulfillment of its open space policy under the Open-Space Easement Act in what Senator Dunlap, in a June 22, 1977, press release, called "the incentive and commitment" of nonprofit organizations to make it work. Not only was it hoped that local land trusts would prove better promoters of the open space easement program than local governments, but landowners were expected to be better disposed to deal with nonprofit organizations than with the politically changeable and therefore distrusted local governments.[40] Secure in the knowledge that a change in local governmental policies could not affect the management or enforcement of easements held by nonprofit organizations, landowners, it was thought, would now want to participate.

While creating a role for nonprofit organizations, the 1977 amendments did not eliminate the governmental planning function of the Act. To qualify for automatic preferential property tax treatment under the Act in its present form, the grant of an easement to a nonprofit organization must still meet with the approval of the county or city in which the property concerned is situated. Approval remains contingent upon a finding of consistency with the local general plan and a finding that the public interest will be served by the easement in question. Nonprofit organizations can accept easements that have not been approved, but automatic use-related property tax assessment under Section 423 of the Revenue and Taxation Code will not be accorded the grantors of such easements. Some degree of cooperativeness on the part of local governments—and a willingness to absorb some loss in tax revenues—remains essential to success of the program.

The 1977 amendments to the Open-Space Easement Act were responsive to the growing awareness in California of the need to preserve local historical, cultural and open space values and the

willingness of private individuals to accept a large measure of responsibility for meeting that need in their own communities. This
trend—evidenced by the emergence of local land trusts—rather than
governmental initiative, will likely provide the impetus for the use of
easements for conservation purposes in California. Although a good
working relationship between local governments and private land
trusts will make the trusts' work easier and more effective, the ability
to act independently of government is perhaps the single most important characteristic of the local land trust. Recognizing this, in
1979, the legislature passed the Conservation Easements Act,[41] making it clear that conservation easements granted to nonprofit conservation organizations—even if outside the governmental approval
channel of the Open-Space Easement Act—create valid, legally enforceable property rights. With this legislation the way was cleared
for nonprofit organizations to be as active in the conservation easement field as their energy and resources permit.

Two important parallel developments complete the picture.
First, in 1978, the voters adopted Proposition 13, a far-reaching tax
abatement measure that has, for the present, significantly reduced the
once urgent role played by property tax relief in open space preservation strategies. Second, in December 1980, an income tax deduction for the donation of qualifying conservation easements to nonprofit organizations—first recognized by the Internal Revenue Service in the late 1960s and codified on a trial basis in 1976—became a
permanent fixture of the Internal Revenue Code. In 1982, an identical
deduction was added to the California Revenue and Taxation Code.
The availability of this deduction creates a strong incentive for the
donation of conservation easements, and it is likely to be the key to
their successful use by private nonprofit organizations, especially in
those cases where Proposition 13 or other factors have made the need
for property tax relief of less immediate concern. With the income tax
deduction as a selling point, nonprofit organizations can make a
persuasive business-minded case for perpetual land protection—
something that is especially important for those individual and
corporate landowners who are not unsympathetic to the conservation cause but need some economic justification for sacrificing the important development rights that a conservation easement restricts.

Income and property tax considerations will have a strong influence on how the conservation easement legislation available in
California will be used. This legislation was not drafted with refer-

ence to the federal tax deduction. For income tax purposes, care must be taken to structure a transaction so as to meet the specific statutory criteria for the federal deduction. As it happens, conformity with a governmental program for open space protection is one approach to satisfying the federal tests for deductibility. Consequently, under the right circumstances, use of the Open-Space Easement Act could prove to be the best way to assure deductibility. Likewise, although the need for it will vary more widely than ever among different landowners after Proposition 13, where property tax relief remains a dominant concern, the Open-Space Easement Act guarantees relief, whereas proof of loss in value is necessary under the Conservation Easements Act. Where, however, the criteria for deductibility can be met without government involvement, and guaranteed use-valuation is not a pressing need, the Conservation Easements Act offers a relatively speedy, noncumbersome way to accomplish the goals of land conservation independent of governmental participation.

As the established conservation organizations and the new land trusts become more familiar with these tools for saving land, the relative merits of the Open-Space Easement Act and the Conservation Easements Act will become apparent. Emerging as it does out of more than twenty years of legislative background, the real history of conservation and open space easements in California has yet to be made.

SUMMARY OF THE KEY LEGISLATION

The Open-Space Easement Act of 1974 and the Conservation Easements Act of 1979 together form the foundation of the easement approach to land conservation in California. Although practically any kind of conservation value can be protected under either one, the Open-Space Easement Act requires the participation of local government—if only to approve an easement granted to a nonprofit conservation organization—whereas an easement granted under the Conservation Easements Act is purely a creature of private law and need entail no governmental involvement. The circumstances of a given transaction will dictate which type of easement should be used.

A third alternative is the Scenic Easement Deed Act of 1959. This Act, the first piece of conservation easement legislation to be enacted, empowers local governments to acquire easements for conservation purposes outside the planning structure of the Open-Space

Easement Act. Whether local governments would ever choose to use this power, given the greater procedural security of the Open-Space Easement Act, is uncertain. However, the Scenic Easement Deed Act remains available should circumstances warrant its use.

A final alternative for the protection of certain open space land uses is the Williamson Act of 1965. The Williamson Act is closely related to the Open-Space Easement Act and serves a similar function but with primary, though not exclusive, focus on agricultural lands. Since 1977, the Williamson Act has provided that an open space easement may be substituted for a Williamson Act contract if the parties so choose. The Williamson Act contract technique has been far more widely used than the easement approach, and local governments are more familiar with it. However, the easement approach is emphasized here because it is readily adaptable to the needs of private parties and because it seems to offer, in the hands of those committed to making it work, the best hope short of full fee purchase for long-term land preservation. Nevertheless, there may be situations in which the Williamson Act contract method would present the best solution to a given land conservation problem, and its availability should not be overlooked. Following is a brief summary of these four Acts.

Open-Space Easement Act of 1974
(Gov't Code §§ 51070–51097)

The Open-Space Easement Act of 1974 is, schematically at least, the principal piece of legislation available for protection of open space in California. In spite of its prominent position in the scheme of things, both local governments and landowners have been reluctant to use it. Its availability since 1977 for use by nonprofit organizations and recent changes in federal tax law may combine, however, to make it an important vehicle for open space land conservation in the future.[42]

The Open-Space Easement Act provides a durable method for the protection of open space lands through the imposition of binding use restrictions. Participation in the Open-Space Easement Act program is entirely voluntary. Economic incentive for participation is supplied by the promise of property tax relief and, under certain circumstances, the probable availability of state and federal income tax deductions. The Act provides a means by which, in exchange for an easement granted either in perpetuity or for as few as ten years to a local government or a qualified nonprofit organization, a landowner can obtain use-related property tax assessment on his lands. For a nonprofit organization to qualify to hold an open space easement, it must have a letter of determination from the IRS that it is a 501(c)(3) organization under the Internal Revenue Code and have open space preservation as a stated purpose in its Articles of Incorporation (§ 51075(f)).

The Act is not technical in defining an easement. Any right or interest granted by deed or other instrument that imposes express limitations on the use of open space land for the purpose of preserving for "public use or enjoyment" its "natural or scenic character" can qualify as an open space easement (§ 51075(d)). In the Act's definition, the term "natural" appears to have been loosely employed. When construed to be consistent with the definition provided for open space land (§ 51075(a)) and the criteria for governmental approval of an easement (§ 51084), it seems merely to indicate the opposite of "improved," in the sense of built upon—that is, natural means open. Land devoted to an open space use, as defined in the Act, is "natural" even if that use should involve the managed production of resources such as crops, timber or minerals (§§ 51084 and 65560). As for the requirement that an easement preserve open space land for "public use or enjoyment," again the meaning is broad. By granting an open space easement to a local government or nonprofit organization, a landowner in effect dedicates the open space character of his land to the public (§ 51081), and such dedication must serve the public interest (§ 51084). However, the Act contains no requirement of public access.

The only mandatory requirement concerning the content of the easement document itself is that it contain a covenant running with the land—and therefore enforceable against the grantor and all subsequent owners of the property—that the landowner will not construct or permit the construction of any improvements not consistent with the easement and not expressly provided for in the instrument (§ 51075(d)).

Open space easements are available to protect any area of land or water that is "essentially unimproved and devoted to an open space use" (§ 51075(a)). Open space use is defined at Government Code Section 65560 (Planning and Zoning Law), and this definition is incorporated in the Open-Space Easement Act at Section 51075(a). The definition is comprehensive. Land devoted to virtually any conceivable open space use is eligible for protection under the Open-Space Easement Act if protecting it is determined to be in the public interest. To indicate the scope of the Act, the following is a partial list of uses included: (1) preservation of natural resources, including plant and animal life, fish and wildlife habitat, ecological study areas, rivers and bays, coastline and watersheds; (2) managed production of resources, including forest, range, agricultural and mineral resources, commercial fisheries and ground water recharge areas; (3) outdoor recreation, including the pursuit of outstanding scenic, historic or cultural values, the use of parks, river and shoreline access and scenic highway corridors; (4) public health and safety, including special management to regulate hazardous conditions posed by flood plains, earthquake faults and unstable soil and to protect and enhance air and water quality (§§ 51075(a) and 65560).

As well as serving the need for a land protection mechanism that is less susceptible to change than zoning, the Open-Space Easement Act is intended to be a flexible tool for effectuating local planning decisions. For this reason, the Open-Space Easement Act is linked to the planning and zoning provisions of the Government Code. No open space easement can be viewed in isolation. Adoption of an open space plan by a city or county is a prerequisite to use of the open space easement technique (§ 51080), and consistency with an area's general plan, including, of course, the mandatory open space element, is essential (§§ 51084 and 65300 et seq.). Whether the grantee of an open space easement is to be a local government entity or a nonprofit organization, the grant of an easement must be reviewed and accepted or approved by the local governing body in consultation with its planning commission before the grantor can become eligible for the property tax benefits provided by the Act (§§ 51083–51085).

The approval process vests broad discretion in the governmental body reviewing the easement. Approval, by resolution, must be based on the dual premise that preserving the open space in question is both consistent with the general plan and in the best interest of the jurisdiction involved (§ 51084). At least one of the following must obtain to support a finding that an easement is in the "best interest" of the city or county affected: (1) the land involved has scenic value, or is valuable as watershed or as a wildlife preserve; (2) retention of the land as open space will "add to the amenities of living in neighboring urbanized areas or will help preserve the rural character of the area in which the land is located"; or (3) "the public interest will otherwise be served in a manner . . . consistent with the purposes of [the Act] and section 8 of Article XIII" of the California Constitution (§ 51084). These criteria are broad enough to permit approval of any bona fide open space easement, and once an easement is approved, the resolution of the governing body approving it establishes a conclusive presumption that the stated criteria have been met (§ 51084). Upon acceptance or approval of an open space easement, the clerk of the governing body records it in the office of the county recorder to impart notice to all of the restrictions imposed on the land in question (§ 51087).

What gives muscle to the Open-Space Easement Act is the fact that once a county or city has accepted or approved an open space easement, it may not issue any building permit for any structure that would violate the terms of the easement (§ 51086). Any threatened construction, development or other activity in violation of the easement must be enjoined by the county, city or qualified nonprofit grantee involved. If a county or city itself violates or fails to enforce an easement, any local landowner or resident may sue to enforce it and, if he prevails, recoup his costs of suit, including attorney's fees (§ 51086).

An open space easement may be granted in perpetuity or for a term of not less than ten years (§§ 51070 and 51081). If a term easement is granted, the Act provides that the full term will be automatically renewed each year unless a notice of nonrenewal is given in timely fashion by either party to the easement instrument (§§ 51081 and 51091). Once notice of nonrenewal is given, the easement remains in full force until the stated term has expired—at minimum, nine years. Nonrenewal by a nonprofit grantee must be approved by the county or city in which the land lies following the procedure outlined below for abandonment (§ 51090). There is, however, no provision for public testing of a nonrenewal initiated by a city or county. A decision not to renew is solely within the discretion of the governing body.

The only way that an open space easement can be terminated other than by expiration of the stated term following a notice of nonrenewal is by abandonment (§ 51093). Abandonment proceedings can be initiated only by petition of the landowner-grantor; the grantee—whether a county, city or nonprofit organization—can take no steps to abandon an easement except at the grantor's request. Ap-

24

proval of abandonment will not be given lightly. An easement granted to a nonprofit organization cannot be abandoned without the approval of its governing board. If the nonprofit organization approves, the landowner must then petition the governing body of the city or county in whose jurisdiction the land lies for approval, just as he is required to do in cases where a governmental entity is the grantee. As stated in Section 51093(a), approval is by resolution based on finding all of the following:

> (1) That no public purpose described in Section 51084 [governing the original approval of the easement] will be served by keeping the land as open space; and
> (2) That the abandonment is not inconsistent with the purposes of [the Act]; and
> (3) That the abandonment is consistent with the local general plan; and
> (4) That the abandonment is necessary to avoid a substantial financial hardship to the landowner due to involuntary factors unique to him.

The abandonment criteria, notably numbers (1) and (4), are as strict as the easement acceptance or approval criteria are relaxed. The governmental body's discretion to approve an abandonment is well confined. Prior to adopting a resolution of abandonment, the governing body of the city or county in question must refer the matter to its planning commission for a public hearing and report on the question of consistency with the general plan. The governing body itself must also hold at least one public hearing on the abandonment issue. If, after all that, abandonment is approved, a nonwaivable abandonment fee of 12½ percent of the fair market value of the property (valued without restrictions) must be paid by the landowner before an abandonment becomes effective. The fee is nondeductible and cannot be added to the basis of the property.[43]

Although abandonment, according to the terms of the Act, can be initiated only by a landowner, there is the practical possibility that de facto abandonment could occur if a nonprofit grantee were to go out of existence. The Open-Space Easement Act does not address this possibility. One solution to this problem may be the careful drafting of the easement instrument to provide for a successor in the event the grantee should cease to exist. Case law in California provides additional backup. A court will appoint a successor to the assets of a charitable organization if it should fail, through dissolution or otherwise, to carry out its charitable purpose.[44] Assuming that in most cases a successor can be found willing and able to take on the burden of maintaining an open space easement, de facto abandonment of an open space easement should be no more than an extremely remote possibility.

The Act is likewise silent on the question of the transferability of open space easements. Since the perceived distrust of government on the part of landowners was one motivation for amending the Act to make nonprofit organizations eligible recipients of open space easements, it would to some extent defeat the amendment to allow transfers from nonprofit organizations to governmental entities. There is nothing in either the letter or spirit of the Act, however, to prevent transfers going the other way.

A local government's acceptance or approval of an open space easement can never be used, intentionally or otherwise, to reduce the cost to government of a later condemnation of the land covered by easement. If an easement is donated to a governmental entity or nonprofit organization, and any entity with the power of eminent domain later seeks to condemn the land under easement, the easement will terminate automatically at the time of filing of the complaint in condemnation and the landowner will be entitled to compensation for the full fair market value of his property as if it had never been burdened by the easement (§ 51095).

Lands subject to open space easements created in accordance with the Open-Space Easement Act are deemed "enforceably restricted" within the meaning of Article XIII, Section 8 of the California Constitution (§ 51096). The legislature has provided that they be assessed for property tax purposes according to the capitalization of income method.[45] Originally, this feature was thought to be all that was necessary to create a sufficient incentive for landowners to participate in the open space easement program. Since the enactment of the Open-Space Easement Act, however, Proposition 13 has intervened to give landowners respite from the intense pressure of exorbitant property tax burdens. But this relief, except for those lands that do not change ownership, will be only temporary. The property tax abatement element of the Open-Space Easement Act should become increasingly more important as time passes. Meanwhile, landowners may be attracted to the Open-Space Easement Act because of its potential usefulness under the new federal tax provisions.[46]

Finally, it is important to note the relationship of the Open-Space Easement Act of 1974 to the Open-Space Easement Act of 1969. Under the Open-Space Easement Act of 1969 the minimum term for an easement was twenty years (with no automatic extension), and abandonment could be initiated only by the city or county. A waivable abandonment fee equal to 12½ percent of the full value of the land was to be payable as deferred taxes (deductible) upon abandonment. Local governments were to receive subventions from the state for lost revenues due to property tax reductions resulting from placing lands under open space easements.[47] The 1974 Act reduced the minimum term of an easement from twenty to ten years, provided for annual automatic extensions, allowed for abandonment at the behest of the landowner rather than the local government entity, made the abandonment fee mandatory and nondeductible and eliminated the subvention program for easements granted after December 31, 1974. The Open-Space Easement Act of 1969 remains applicable to that limited number of easements granted under its terms prior to the 1974 Act. In all other respects, it is superseded by the 1974 Act.

California Conservation Easements Act of 1979
(Civ. Code §§ 815–816)

As conservation organizations such as The Trust for Public Land, The Nature Conservancy and numerous local land trusts throughout the United States have been proving for several years now, the conservation easement is well suited to the needs of the financially strapped but deeply committed private conservation movement. Recourse to the easement device as an alternative to outright acquisition of land greatly enlarges the scope of what private conservation organizations can accomplish. However, the Open-Space Easement Act, were it the only avenue available for use of the conservation easement device, would unnecessarily limit what private organizations could do with the easement technique in California because of its insistence on governmental participation in the process. In California, the validity of conservation easements created by private parties outside the Open-Space Easement Act was, prior to the Conservation Easements Act, open to question. The conservation easement was a new twist on an ancient form. It had never been tested in court, and there was concern that it was perhaps too novel to be enforceable under existing law.[48] Landowners and conservation organizations wanted to use it but were hesitant. To allay doubt concerning the enforceability of conservation easements and to give full play to the desire of conservation organizations to make use of them, the legislature passed the Conservation Easements Act of 1979.

The Conservation Easements Act is not linked to any particular program for open space protection. It establishes no new system of incentives and deterrents aimed at controlling development, and it does not relate to any governmental planning function. What it does is to assure the enforceability of conservation easements through the statutory removal of common law impediments to their enforceability.

Under our legal tradition, the affirmative easement (the right to some specific use of the property of another) is an important and well-protected type of interest in real property. However, negative easements (i.e., easements prohibiting some use of land) are disfavored because they run counter to a strong common law preference for the free use of land. Generally, only three basic types of negative easements are recognized: prevention of interference with (1) light, air or view, (2) the lateral and subjacent support of adjoining land and (3) the uninterrupted flow of water. Agreements to refrain from certain uses of land that fall outside these limited categories will most often be classified as restrictive covenants or equitable servitudes and will be required to meet a number of rather involved tests in order to be upheld against subsequent transferees of the burdened property.[49] In addition, while an affirmative easement may run either to the benefit of another piece of property (called an "appurtenant" easement) or to the benefit of an individual (called an easement "in gross"), a negative easement, or for that matter a restrictive covenant or equitable servitude, must run to the benefit of other land to be enforceable against anyone other than the original parties to the agreement.

Conservation easements of an affirmative type (for example, those that allow recreation or educational pursuits or create access rights) face no real difficulties under these rules. However, conservation easements that are negative, and particularly conservation easements that are both negative and in gross, fall outside the accepted common law categories, thereby raising doubts as to their long-range validity. In order to prevent uncertainty from impeding the development of the conservation easement method for preserving open space resources, the Conservation Easements Act makes the common law distinctions inapplicable to conservation easements and clarifies the remedies available for their enforcement.

In the Conservation Easements Act, a conservation easement is defined broadly to encompass any restriction on real property imposed for conservation purposes. Technical distinctions between easements, covenants and conditions are eliminated:

§ 815.1. Conservation easement

For the purposes of this chapter, "conservation easement" means any limitation in a deed, will, or other instrument in the form of an easement, restriction, covenant, or condition, which is or has been executed by or on behalf of the owner of the land subject to such easement and is binding upon successive owners of such land, and the purpose of which is to retain land predominantly in its natural, scenic, historical, agricultural, forested, or open-space condition.

All common law impediments to such an interest are removed by legislative fiat. The Act provides as follows:

1. A conservation easement is an *interest in real property*, even though it may be negative in character (§ 815.2(a) and (c)) [a conservation easement is enforceable as an easement even though it may not fit the established categories for easements].

2. It is to be *freely transferable* among qualified holders for the conservation purposes stated in the above definition (§ 815.2(a)).

3. It is *not* to be deemed *personal* in nature (§ 815.2(c)) [a conservation easement is binding on whoever owns the restricted land, not just on the original parties to the agreement].

4. Lack of *privity* of contract, lack of *benefit* to particular land, or lack of a recitation in the deed that it is intended to *run with the land* do not affect its enforceability (§ 815.7(a)) [a conservation easement runs with the land rather than the contracting parties even though it does not meet the tests for a running covenant].

5. A conservation easement is enforceable by *injunction* at the behest of the grantor or the holder of the easement. In addition to injunctive relief, money damages also will lie, not only for the costs of restoration but for the loss of scenic, aesthetic or environmental values (§ 815.7(b) and (c)) [although damages might, under certain circumstances, be the only remedy available for enforcing a restric-

tive covenant, injunctive relief is available for the enforcement of a conservation easement in order to make it fully protective of the conservation values involved].

In order to assure that conservation easements are used for conservation purposes as intended, Section 815 stipulates that only a state or local governmental entity or a tax-exempt nonprofit organization qualified under Section 501(c)(3) of the Internal Revenue Code may acquire and hold them (§ 815.3). For a nonprofit organization to be eligible it must have "as its *primary purpose* the preservation, protection, or enhancement of land in its natural, scenic, historical, agricultural, forested, or open-space condition or use" (§ 815.3(a) [emphasis added]). In addition, conservation easements must be perpetual in duration (§ 815.2(b)).

Freed from the limitations imposed by the common law, the conservation easement emerges as a highly flexible tool for achieving land conservation in a relatively noncumbersome way. The form of a conservation easement can be molded to fit the situation at hand without undue concern for formalities. As the Act states: "the particular characteristics of a conservation easement shall be those granted or specified in the instrument creating or transferring the easement" (§ 815.2(d)). Some expression of intent to bind successive owners of the burdened land (§ 815.1) and notice by recordation (§ 815.5) are all that is necessary to insure that a conservation easement will run with the land in perpetuity. To insure that new technicalities do not spring up to replace the common law impediments removed by the Act, the legislature has instructed the courts that Section 815 is to be liberally construed (§ 816).

OBSERVATIONS

1981 Amendment. As originally enacted, the Conservation Easements Act applied only to conservation easements held by qualified nonprofit conservation organizations. The enforceability of conservation easements held by federal, state and, when taken outside the Open-Space Easement Act, local governmental entities was still open to question. The Act was amended in 1981 to include "the state or any city, county, city and county, district, or other state or local governmental entity, if otherwise authorized to acquire and hold title to real property" as authorized holders of conservation easements (§ 815.3(b)).[50] Amended Section 815.3(b) specifies, however, that conservation easements may only be voluntarily conveyed; they may not be exacted from landowners in return for any government-issued entitlement.

The 1981 amendment to the Conservation Easements Act makes it clear that, when using easements for conservation purposes, local governments as well as nonprofit organizations are to have the option of proceeding within or without the local planning context of the Open-Space Easement Act. In addition, state agencies, such as the State Coastal Conservancy, and local and regional park and open space districts, among others, can now accept conservation easements without fear of challenge as to their validity. Only federal agencies remain outside the ambit of the new conservation easement law in California. At a time when the federal government is espousing a less-than-fee approach to carrying out its land conservation duties,[51] this may prove an unfortunate omission.

Property Taxes. The favorable property tax consequences bestowed on the grantor of an open space easement under the Open-Space Easement Act of 1974 are conspicuously absent from the Conservation Easements Act of 1979. Section 815 addresses enforceability only; other policy questions remain unresolved. Whether this will inhibit its use remains to be seen. Post–Prop 13, a landowner is likely to be more concerned with the availability of an estate or income tax deduction than a reduction in property taxes. Nevertheless, if a before-and-after donation valuation yields a positive value for the interest given up, that reduction in value could lead to a lower assessment valuation depending on the base year value used in assessing the property and the receptivity of the local assessor.[52]

Damages for Loss of Environmental Values. Although the Conservation Easements Act contemplates, in addition to injunctive relief, the recovery of money damages for injury to a conservation easement—including the scenic, aesthetic and environmental values protected by the easement—it is not clear how such intangible interests are to be reduced to monetary equivalents. Accurate valuation of such interests has proven to be a problem in the sphere of cost/benefit analysis both because they are of a highly subjective nature and because the benefit derived from them is so broadly dispersed among the public at large. It is fair to say that no truly satisfactory methodology for measuring the monetary worth of environmental and aesthetic values exists. Nevertheless, by indicating that the loss of environmental values may be compensated, the legislature has delegated to the courts the power to find a way to insure that the intangible values that conservation easements serve will not be slighted by economic analysis.

Modification and Termination. One serious deficiency of the Conservation Easements Act is that it is silent regarding modification and termination of a conservation easement. The first draft of the bill recognized the need to provide for extinguishment but left open the standards and procedure to be followed.[53] In the process of strengthening the Act's requirement of perpetuity, all reference to termination was subsequently dropped.

The fact that an easement is intended to be perpetual in duration does not guarantee that it will be so in fact. Perpetuity in the relationships of people to land is never absolute. Change is always a factor. Circumstances might arise to nullify the specific purpose for which an easement was granted, or the holder of an easement might abandon it. Presumably, a court could step in to modify or terminate an easement when the situation warranted it, but the absence of any legislative guidance gives the courts more discretion to determine what circumstances justify modification or termination than may be desirable.

The core of the problem is that, left to themselves, the courts may apply a more lenient test for the extinguishment of conservation easements than they apply to common law easements. Under the so-called doctrine of changed conditions, a court can modify or terminate a restrictive covenant or equitable servitude when, in the court's opinion, changes in the neighborhood of a restricted property, including changes that have dramatically altered its economic value, have made the restriction obsolete.[54] For example, a court might allow the commercial development of a property restricted by covenant for residential use when the area around the property has become predominantly commercial over time. A common law easement, on the other hand, can only be modified or extinguished by the act or omission of its holder—as, for example, by release, merger, abandonment or prescription.[55] The only exception to this is where an easement is created for a specific purpose and the purpose is either fully and finally accomplished or, for some reason, has become impossible to accomplish.[56] For example, an easement to take water from a well terminates when, for whatever reason, the well runs dry.

It is one thing to remove the use restrictions imposed by a conservation easement when they no longer serve the purpose for which they were imposed. Protecting the habitat of an endangered species makes no sense if, despite such efforts, the species becomes extinct. It is another thing, however, to extinguish a still viable conservation easement because changes in the use pattern of surrounding lands have made the land under easement a local anomaly. The continued enforcement of the easement under such circumstances might be more important than ever. It is conceivable, however, that in the absence of legislative guidance, a court might apply the doctrine of changed conditions to terminate an otherwise viable easement that has become, to some degree, an economic hardship to the owner of restricted land. Whether a court should be permitted to do so is an important policy question still to be faced.

The Conservation Easements Act's silence regarding termination is problematic in another respect. Even if a conservation easement can only be terminated in the same way as a common law easement, the possibility always exists that the holder of a conservation easement might abandon it either by failing to enforce it or by going out of existence itself. Although there may be good reason to extinguish a common law easement under some circumstances, to allow extinguishment by abandonment of an otherwise viable conservation easement would defeat the purposes of the Conservation Easements Act. Proper drafting of an easement may alleviate this concern. For example, it may be advisable to insert a deed provision for transfer of the easement to another qualified holder in the event that the grantee organization should fail to enforce it or cease to exist. However, leaving it to the parties in every case obviously invites problems. Even though a court could appoint a successor to the original easement holder, considerable damage might be done to the resource values involved before a court would have the opportunity to act.

Although perpetual in the abstract, conservation easements will require continuing, energetic "maintenance" on the part of their holders to make them perpetual in fact. Litigation concerning the questions of modification and termination is certainly foreseeable. A development-minded successor may one day replace the conservation-minded grantor. It is not clear from the Act that he could not use the lever of "changed conditions" to roll away the conservation easement, nor is there any assurance that a conservation organization holder will always be there to prevent him from trying.

Scenic Easement Deed Act of 1959
(Gov't Code §§ 6950-6954)

This was the first piece of open space easement legislation not only in California but in the United States.[57] The Act established open space preservation as a public purpose and authorizes cities and counties to acquire fee or lesser interests in real property for the purpose of conserving open space. Open space is defined in Section 6954 of the Act as:

> Any space or area characterized by (1) great natural scenic beauty or (2) whose existing openness, natural condition, or present state of use, if retained, would enhance the present or potential value of abutting or surrounding urban development, or would maintain or enhance the conservation of natural or scenic resources.

The Act has gone virtually unused, in large part, it is thought, because no direction was given to local governments for its use and no tax incentives were built into it to attract potential grantors.[58] The Open-Space Easement Act of 1969 was enacted to remedy the disuse of the 1959 Act by providing both the clear direction for use of the easement technique and the property tax incentives that were lacking in the 1959 Act.[59] However, the 1959 Act has never been repealed, and it presents an alternative by which cities and counties can, if they so desire, bypass the procedural requirements of the Open-Space Easement Act to accept conservation easements. The Conservation Easements Act, as amended in 1981, assures the enforceability of conservation easements granted to local governmental entities outside the Open-Space Easement Act.

Land Conservation Act of 1965—Williamson Act
(Gov't Code §§ 51200-51295)

Although the Williamson Act is not, properly speaking, open space easement legislation, anyone considering the easement approach to land conservation must take the Williamson Act contract approach into account as well. Although its effectiveness is debated and many have concluded that it has not achieved any significant conservation of those prime agricultural lands most vulnerable to development,[60] the Williamson Act, due to the extensive use to which it has been put, remains the most important piece of land conservation legislation presently available in California. Several of its features were copied in the Open-Space Easement Act. In reviewing the options available for protecting sensitive land resources without undue economic loss, a landowner who is eligible for Williamson Act treatment should, depending on his needs, consider the Williamson Act as an important alternative to the open space or conservation easement approach.

The Williamson Act provides a means whereby landowners whose lands fall within city- or county-designated agricultural preserve areas may contract with their local city or county governments to restrict the use of their lands to agricultural or certain other open space uses in exchange for use-related property tax assessment valuation. Contracts are for a minimum term of ten years, with provision for annual automatic renewal to maintain the original term in effect on a continuing basis until either party gives notice of intent not to renew (§ 51244). Cancellation is allowed only if consistent with the purposes of the Act or otherwise in the public interest, both of which grounds are carefully and precisely delineated in the Act (§ 51282). Upon cancellation, a landowner is required to pay a deductible cancellation fee, which may be waived by the city or county under certain prescribed conditions, and similarly deductible and waivable additional deferred taxes (§§ 51283–51283.1). The value for tax assessment purposes of property subject to a Williamson Act contract is determined according to the capitalization of income method set forth at Section 423 of the Revenue and Taxation Code.

Although originally designed specifically for the protection of agricultural lands, the Williamson Act was later amended to encompass certain other nonagricultural uses of open space. The scope of the Act now includes the following open space land uses: recreation, scenic highway corridors, wildlife habitat, salt ponds, managed wetlands and submerged areas (§ 51205).

In 1977, the Williamson Act was amended to provide that the parties to a contract may rescind the contract by mutual agreement and substitute for it an open space easement agreement pursuant to the Open-Space Easement Act of 1974 (§ 51255). The extent to which a substitution can be used to alter the terms of the original agreement, and whether at the time of substitution or at some future time a nonprofit organization could replace a city or county as a party, is not clear. However, this amendment is indicative of how closely related the Williamson Act contract and the open space easement are.

Where property tax relief is the primary motivation for a land-owner in seeking to restrict the use of his land, either the Williamson Act or the Open-Space Easement Act may serve his needs, depending on where his land is situated, the use to which the land is being put, the attitude of local government personnel toward the two approaches and the relative effect of the two Acts' differing provisions concerning entering into a restriction, cancellation or abandonment and the fees involved. However, where more than property tax relief motivates a landowner's decision to restrict his property—where a desire to preserve the land in perpetuity and to obtain corresponding income or estate tax deductions are factors—the Williamson Act contract is likely to prove less adaptable than the conservation easement to the requirements of the state and federal tax laws.

RELATED LEGISLATION

Article XIII, Section 8 (Formerly Article XXVIII) of the California Constitution

Article XXVIII of the California Constitution was approved by the electorate as Proposition 3 in 1966. Article XXVIII provided the underpinnings for the property tax relief embodied in the Williamson Act and the Open-Space Easement Act. It freed open space legislation from the strictures of mandatory market value assessment. By its terms, Article XXVIII empowered the legislature to define open space, specify what constituted an enforceable restriction on open space lands and provide that enforceably restricted open space lands be valued "for property tax purposes only on a basis that is consistent with . . . [their] restrictions and uses." On the authority of Article XXVIII, the legislature added Sections 421–425 to the Revenue and Taxation Code to codify the capitalization of income method of assessment for qualifying open space lands.[61]

In 1974, as part of the legislature's continuing constitutional revision project, Article XXVIII was repealed and, in substance, moved to Article XIII, Section 8 in order to consolidate all provisions dealing with property tax assessment in one article.[62] The original intent of Article XXVIII, to facilitate the preservation of open space, is carried over into Article XIII, Section 8, and it is that Article that now provides the authority for the tax relief embodied in the Williamson Act and the Open-Space Easement Act. Article XIII, Section 8 was amended in 1976 to provide for similar use-related valuation for enforceably restricted historical properties. The legislature has used the power granted to it by Article XIII, Section 8 sparingly.

1970 Amendments to the Planning and Zoning Law: Open Space Land (Gov't Code §§ 65560–65570) and Open Space Zoning (Gov't Code §§ 65910–65912)

These additions to the California Planning and Zoning Law were a partial response to the final report made by the Joint Committee on Open Space Land in 1970, pointing out the need for and recommending implementation of a comprehensive statewide policy of open space land planning and use. The Open Space Amendments required every city and county in the state to prepare a local open space plan for review by the secretary of the State Resources Agency by December 31, 1973 (§ 65563). Each plan was required to contain an action program for its implementation (§ 65564). All city and county actions, building permits, subdivision maps and zoning ordinances are to be consistent with the local open space plan.

To complement the open space plan, every city and county was also required to adopt an open space zoning ordinance before December 31, 1973 (§ 65910; authority to regulate open space by ordinance was granted at § 65850). Variances from the terms of the ordinance are to be allowed only when necessary, because of special circumstances applicable to a property, to prevent the deprivation of privileges enjoyed by identically zoned neighboring properties (§ 65911). No special privileges are to be allowed, and Section 65911 is to be "literally and strictly interpreted and enforced."

These amendments are important for conservation easement purposes because no easement can be accepted or approved by a city or county under the Open-Space Easement Act of 1974 prior to adoption of a local open space plan (§ 51080). In addition, the comprehensive definition of open space at Section 65560 of the Planning Section is incorporated in the Open-Space Easement Act (§ 51075(a)), potentially giving that Act a very broad scope.

California Timberland Productivity Act of 1982
(Formerly Z'berg-Warren-Keene-Collier Forest Taxation Reform Act of 1976) (Gov't Code §§ 51100–51155)

The Forest Taxation Reform Act of 1976, recently renamed the California Timberland Productivity Act of 1982,[63] operates much like the Williamson Act except for the all-important difference that participation is mandatory rather than voluntary. It is the only mandatory statewide open space program in California. Its purpose is to maintain the state's threatened timberland base and to insure the long-term productivity of its forest resources (§§ 51101–51103). Timberland is defined as land used for growing and harvesting timber (capable of an average annual volume of at least fifteen cubic feet of wood fiber per acre) and for compatible uses including watershed or wildlife management (§ 51100(g) and (h)). Under the terms of the Act, all timberland is zoned in timberland production zones (TPZ's, formerly called timberland preserve zones) and the use of such land is thereafter restricted to the production of timber or compatible uses for a period of ten years, subject to annual automatic renewal. Timberland is assessed for property tax purposes according to a grading system based on site quality and operability, and the standing timber itself is exempt from property taxation.[64] Timberland production zoning has gradually replaced the use of the Williamson Act agricultural preserve for protecting qualifying timberland (§§ 51110, 51246 and 51282.5).

Open Space Subventions, 1972
(Gov't Code §§ 16140–16154)

These sections provide for partial reimbursement by the state of revenues foregone by local governments as a result of their participation in the Williamson Act or, before January 1, 1975, either the Scenic Easement Deed Act or the Open-Space Easement Act of 1969.[65] Participating cities and counties are eligible for subventions at varying rates depending on the location, agricultural quality or statewide significance of restricted lands within their jurisdictions (§ 16142). No subvention payments are available for lands restricted under the Open-Space Easement Act of 1974 (§ 16141) or the Conservation Easements Act. The principal benefit of the tax subsidy provided by the open space subvention program accrues to local governments using the Williamson Act.

Of note is the fact that the open space subvention sections of the Code provide the state with backup power to enforce open space restrictions. The secretary of the State Resources Agency may request the attorney general to enforce, by injunction or specific performance, restrictions on land for which subventions have been given (§ 16147).

Open Space Amendments to Regional Park Districts Law, 1975 and 1982 (Pub. Res. Code §§ 5500–5595); Recreation and Park Districts (Pub. Res. Code §§ 5780–5791)

Sections 5500–5595 of the Public Resources Code, as amended, authorize the creation of regional park and open space districts by neighboring cities whether in the same or different counties and set forth the procedures governing and the powers of such districts. Among the express powers of such park and open space districts is the power to acquire real and personal property and "rights in real and personal property" by any means including condemnation (§§ 5540–5542). The 1982 amendment to Section 5540 specifies that open space easements executed and accepted by a district are to be deemed enforceably restricted within the meaning of Article XIII, Section 8 of the California Constitution, with the result that open space lands subject to easements granted to regional park and open space districts are now qualified for automatic use-valuation for property tax assessment purposes. Section 421 of the Revenue and Taxation Code likewise was amended in 1982 to reflect this change.[66]

A local city or county recreation and park district created under Sections 5780–5791 may likewise, by any means including condemnation, obtain real or personal property "or any interest therein" for the benefit of the district (§ 5782.5(b) and (c)). This authorization makes local recreation and park districts eligible to acquire and hold conservation easements under amended Section 815.3(b) of the Conservation Easements Act.

Roberti-Z'berg Urban Open Space and Recreation Program Act, 1976 (Pub. Res. Code §§ 5620–5632)

This Act establishes a funded state grant program, administered by the State Department of Parks and Recreation, providing for grants to cities, counties and regional and local park districts to be used for the acquisition and development of recreational or open space lands and facilities.

Open Space Maintenance Act, 1965
(Gov't Code §§ 50575–50628)

This Act provides a means by which local governments may form open space maintenance districts for the purpose of levying a special annual assessment on real property within a district to pay the costs of maintaining and operating the district's open areas. This Act is directly linked by its terms to the Scenic Easement Deed Act and is intended to provide a means of maintaining open space areas acquired under that Act (§ 50582). The prime concern of the Act is to insure that open space for which local governments are responsible is properly maintained in order to prevent the hazards of fire, erosion and flooding, with particular emphasis on fire control in open areas under natural vegetative cover. Because the Scenic Easement Deed Act has received little, if any, use, the Open Space Maintenance Act has been of little practical importance to date.

Absolute Immunity of Public Land Trusts from Personal Injury Liability on State-sanctioned Public Access Lands; Qualified Immunity for Recreation on Private Lands (Gov't Code § 831.5 and Civ. Code § 846)

Sections 831.2 and 831.4 of the Government Code provide absolute immunity to all public entities and their employees from liability to any person for injuries caused by any natural condition existing on unimproved public land. The purpose of these sections is to prevent the threat of tort liability from constricting the number and quality of opportunities available for park, recreation and open space activities on publicly owned lands. Assumption of the risk of injury on public lands is part of the price the public pays for the benefit of access to public lands.[67]

In 1980, the legislature added Section 831.5 to the Government Code to extend the governmental immunity of Sections 831.2 and 831.4 to "public land trusts" under certain specified conditions. The term *public land trust* is not defined in Section 831.5, but the prerequisites for immunity are stated to be: (1) nonprofit status under Section 501(c) of the Internal Revenue Code and (2) express provision in the organization's articles of incorporation that "the conservation of land for public access, agricultural, scientific, historical, educational, recreational, scenic or open space opportunities" are among its principal charitable purposes. If such an organization enters into an agreement with the State Coastal Conservancy or the State Public Works Board or its designee to provide nondiscriminatory public access consistent with resource protection, it will be treated as a public entity for the purpose of shielding it from tort liability under Sections 831.2 and 831.4. As Section 831.5(a) states, this amendment was added to encourage responsible nonprofit organizations to carry out "innovative public access programs" as an alternative to costly public acquisition programs.

Section 831.5 immunity does not extend to all conservation easements where public access is allowed but only to those that are linked to an access agreement with the named state agencies. There is, however, a qualified immunity available to owners of real property interests, including easements, who permit entry for recreational purposes on their lands. Civil Code Section 846, enacted in 1963, provides that, apart from liability for willful or malicious derelictions, an owner of any interest in real property has no duty to keep the premises safe for recreational purposes or to give warning to recreationists of hazardous conditions on the land, whether natural or manmade, except when an express invitation to enter the premises has been extended or where consideration is normally received for the right to enter for recreational purposes. As with Government Code Section 831.5, the purpose of this legislation is to prevent tort liability from becoming a counterproductive barrier to the broadest possible availability of recreational open space.

A holder of a conservation easement with a central public access purpose would do well to seek an agreement with the state under Government Code Section 831.5 to assure insulation from potential tort liability. Where, however, public access for recreation is at most incidental, Civil Code Section 846 should provide sufficient protection against such liability. But a note of caution. The courts, in their solicitude for tort plaintiffs, have tended to construe Section 846 narrowly against the party claiming immunity.[68] It is good practice for conservation organizations in negotiating and drafting conservation easements to allocate to the landowner both the burden of maintaining the property subject to easement and any potential tort liability as well.

Presumptions Affecting the Burden of Proof in Eminent Domain Proceedings (Code of Civ. Proc. §§ 1240.670, 1240.680 and 1240.690)

Lands set aside for open space uses have no immunity from the possibility of condemnation. Public entities empowered to exercise the right of eminent domain may exercise that right even against property, or any interest in property, already appropriated to public use, if the public use for which the property is sought is considered to be "more necessary" than the use to which the property is already being put.[69] However, the legislature has made it more difficult for public entities to condemn certain open space lands. Section 1240.670 of the Code of Civil Procedure provides that property (defined to include any interest in property)[70] owned by nonprofit conservation organizations that is dedicated irrevocably and exclusively to the preservation of native plants, animals, biotic communities or geological or geographical formations of scientific or educational interest and is open to the public subject to reasonable restrictions is presumed already to be appropriated to the "best and most necessary public use." The condemning agency would have the burden of rebutting these presumptions. Likewise, state, regional, county or city park, open space or recreation areas are presumed to be appropriated to the "best and most necessary public use" (Code of Civ. Proc. § 1240.680). Where the State Department of Transportation seeks to acquire property described in Sections 1240.670 and 1240.680 for state highway purposes, the nonprofit or public owner of the property in question must, to preserve the presumption in its favor, bring a timely action for declaratory relief to determine which use is the most necessary public use for the property (§ 1240.690). Although normally a public entity's resolution of necessity is conclusive on issues pertaining to the public necessity of a particular taking,[71] Section 1240.690(c) provides that the State Transportation Commission's resolution of necessity is not conclusive in the declaratory relief proceeding established by that section.

State Coastal Conservancy (Pub. Res. Code §§ 31000-31405); Santa Monica Mountains Conservancy (Pub. Res. Code §§ 33000-33216)

An active, funded, comprehensive state open space program has yet to be inaugurated in California. However, a model for such a program does exist at the present time and is operative within the entire California coastal zone under the authority of the California Coastal Act of 1976.[72] The Coastal Act—and its immediate predecessor, the Coastal Zone Conservation Act, which was enacted by initiative on November 7, 1972—was passed to assure, through the comprehensive planning and rigorous control of land uses, the protection of the coastal zone environment and the "orderly, balanced utilization and conservation of coastal zone resources."[73]

The State Coastal Commission, created by the Coastal Zone Conservation Act, oversees and regulates development of the coastal zone. Predictably, it has been at the center of much controversy in the continuing conflict between private and public rights. Less controversial, but no less important, the State Coastal Conservancy was created by the Coastal Act of 1976 to take the lead role in preserving, restoring and enhancing coastal resource lands (including agricultural lands) and improving public access to them. It is the Conservancy's responsibility to coordinate a program of acquisitions, options, leases, grants, loans, development rights transfers, and agreements pertaining to open space lands and involving extensive interagency cooperation and substantial participation by nonprofit organizations. The Conservancy is designed to play a pioneering role in developing innovative approaches to land conservation in California, and it makes extensive use of, among other techniques, the conservation easement.

The State Coastal Conservancy serves as a short-term repository for lands or partial interests in lands required to be reserved under the Coastal Act or local coastal plans for park or open space uses (§ 31104.1). Backed by the State Public Works Board's power of eminent domain, the Conservancy is authorized to acquire fee or lesser interests in real property in carrying out the purposes of the Act (§§ 31105 and 31106). Specifically, the Conservancy is empowered to acquire fee or lesser interests in agricultural lands and to reconvey such interests to private individuals subject to restrictions to assure their perpetual preservation (§ 31150). Alternatively, the Conservancy can award grants to local public agencies and nonprofit organizations for the purpose of acquiring fee or lesser interests in coastal agricultural lands (§ 31156). The Conservancy can acquire key coastal resource lands and transfer such lands to public agencies or nonprofit organizations (§§ 31350–31355). It can acquire fee or lesser interests in land required for public access to significant coastal resources (§ 31402). It can award grants to public agencies or nonprofit organizations to further conservation purposes within the coastal zone, and in particular to acquire both public coastal accessways (§ 31400.1) and less-than-fee interests on sensitive coastal resource lands (§ 31115). In short, the State Coastal Conservancy is a funded public conservation agency with a strong mandate for the protection of coastal open space resource values. It is an indispensable source of funds and assistance to local governments and nonprofit organizations, offering unprecedented opportunities for public and private sector cooperation.

In 1979, the State Coastal Conservancy was used by the legislature as a model for the creation of the Santa Monica Mountains Conservancy (§ 33000–33216), whose purpose is to coordinate, in cooperation with local governments and the National Park Service, the protection of threatened open space resources within the Santa Monica Mountains. Among the powers of the Santa Monica Mountains Conservancy is the power to acquire, and make grants to local agencies to enable them to acquire, open space lands and interests in land and to serve as a temporary repository for open space lands and interests in land that have been offered for dedication by developers and others.

Keene-Nejedly California Wetlands Preservation Act, 1976 (Pub. Res. Code §§ 5810–5818)

This Act charges the Parks and Recreation and Fish and Game departments to devise and carry out a program "for the acquisition, protection, preservation, restoration and enhancement of wetlands," which the legislature perceived to be of "increasingly critical economic, aesthetic, and scientific value to the people of California" (§§ 5811 and 5814). Significantly, the Act empowers either department, where appropriate, to "acquire interests in real property less than the fee, including, but not limited to, acquisition of development rights" (§ 5813). The Act mandates that the departments, whenever possible, coordinate their efforts with the conservation, recreation and open space plans and programs of local agencies and allows for local management and control of wetlands under certain circumstances (§§ 5815 and 5817).

CHAPTER TWO

TAX INCENTIVES FOR THE DONATION OF CONSERVATION EASEMENTS

For governmental agencies and conservation organizations, the conservation easement represents an important and much needed alternative to the outright ownership and day-to-day management of land for conservation purposes, which often is neither feasible nor desirable. The use of conservation easements, where appropriate, can be a highly efficient means of stretching the limited funds currently available for land conservation. In recognition of this fact and to encourage the donation of conservation easements, federal and state lawmakers have made substantial tax incentives available. On the federal side, these incentives take the form of income and estate tax deductions; on the state side, an income tax deduction and, for open space easements, automatic property tax relief. These incentives are discussed below, with particular emphasis being given to the federal income tax deduction because of the powerful influence it is likely to have on the development of the conservation easement as a significant land conservation device.

FEDERAL TAX LAW

Background of the Federal Income Tax Deduction

The first public recognition that the gift of a conservation easement qualified as a deductible charitable contribution came in 1964 when the Internal Revenue Service issued Revenue Ruling 64–205.[74] The taxpayer in that case donated a perpetual easement to the United States restricting the use of property adjoining a federal highway to preserve its scenic value. The ruling stated that the easement— which contained restrictions on the grantor's use of his property dealing with, among other things, the type and height of buildings allowed, removal of trees, erection of utility lines, dumping of trash, use of signs and allowable parcel size in the event of subdivision—

represented a valuable property right under applicable state law. It followed that, as a donation of value to a qualified organization, the easement ought to be deductible. In 1965, the IRS gave further support to this ruling by issuing an informational news release confirming the availability of income tax deductions for "scenic easements."[75]

Revenue Ruling 64–205 was the only official pronouncement on the subject until the Tax Reform Act of 1969.[76] One of the provisions of the 1969 Act (Section 170(f) of the Internal Revenue Code) attempted to eradicate certain charitable gift shelters considered by the U.S. Treasury Department to be unjustifiable—involving gifts of property in trust and the donation of the *use* of property for a limited time—by tightening the qualifications for gifts in trust and disallowing deductions for contributions to charities of less than a taxpayer's entire interest in property. Exceptions to the entire interest requirement were made for a remainder interest in a personal residence or farm and an "undivided portion of the taxpayer's entire interest in property."[77] By its terms this new provision appeared to have eliminated the deductibility of gifts of easements, but the Conference Committee Report rescued easement gifts by employing the simple expedient of a somewhat awkward fiction: "The conferees on the part of both Houses intend that a gift of an open space easement in gross is to be considered a gift of an undivided interest in the property where the easement is in perpetuity."[78]

The Treasury Department subsequently adopted this expression of congressional intent in its regulations, adding that an easement in gross was a "mere personal interest" unsupported by any dominant estate and giving as an example an easement similar to the one described in Revenue Ruling 64–205.[79] Later, the IRS, in a series of liberal interpretive rulings, significantly expanded the open space easement concept to embrace an affirmative easement for a hiking trail,[80] a façade easement on an historical building[81] and a beach-front easement for use of the public.[82]

Despite these liberal IRS rulings, practitioners were forced to be cautious. The authority for conservation and historic preservation easements was considered precarious at best, lying as it did outside of the Code itself. In many states, where open space easements in gross were not recognized under the applicable real property law, it was impossible to comply strictly with the regulatory definition of a qualifying easement. There was "considerable uncertainty" as to how to proceed, and that uncertainty "had thrown a cloud over the growing use of easements for conservation and historic preservation purposes."[83]

The Tax Reform Act of 1976[84] (as amended by the Tax Reduction and Simplification Act of 1977)[85] sought to remedy the situation by making explicit the deductibility of charitable contributions of less-than-fee interests made for conservation purposes. The following exceptions were added to Section 170(f)(3)(B): "(iii) a lease on, option to purchase, or easement with respect to real property granted in perpetuity[86] to an organization described in subsection (b)(1)(A) exclusively for conservation purposes, or (iv) a remainder interest in real property which is granted to an organization described in subsection (b)(1)(A) exclusively for conservation purposes."

Conservation purposes were defined as follows:

> (C) Conservation purposes defined. For purposes of subparagraph (B), the term "conservation purposes" means—
>> (i) the preservation of land areas for public outdoor recreation or education, or scenic enjoyment;
>> (ii) the preservation of historically important land areas or structures; or
>> (iii) the protection of natural environmental systems.

Although the new statutory exceptions addressed the same area of law that had been governed previously by the undivided interest exception, they did not expressly supersede the latter, and some conservation organizations were inclined to prefer the administrative development of the open space easement exception over the potentially far more rigid new statutory provisions. In addition, the IRS continued to issue private letter rulings based on the undivided interest exception.[87]

Regulations pursuant to the 1976–1977 changes were never promulgated. Although the Conference Committee Report accompanying the new provisions indicated that they were to be liberally construed,[88] the task of drafting workable regulations would have been a difficult one. The regulations would have had to come to grips with numerous problems inherent in the vague statutory criteria. It was not clear, for example, what was intended to be covered under the heading "natural environmental systems" or whether a scenic easement need have a public use aspect, and the legislative history provided no clues. Even more important, the omission of such vital conservation purposes as the protection of timberland, farmland and wetland from the statutory conservation purpose categories left far too broad a discretion in Treasury to determine the deductibility of easements granted for such purposes. If deductions for donations serving these important conservation purposes were to have been disallowed, the potential usefulness of the conservation easement device would have been greatly reduced. The overall effect of the 1976–1977 changes was to bring more uncertainty to the conservation easement area rather than, as was hoped, to dispel that which was already there.

The 1980 Federal Conservation Easement Income Tax Deduction (I.R.C. §§ 170(f)(3)(B) and 170(h))

The 1977 Act placed a "sunset date" (expiration date) of June 14, 1981, on the conservation easement exception. Legislation sponsored by Congressman John Dingell of Michigan and Congressman Andy Jacobs of Indiana to remove this sunset date was passed on December 17, 1980, in the Tax Treatment Extension Act.[89] In addition to removing the sunset date, thereby making the conservation easement deduction a permanent feature of the Internal Revenue Code, the Tax Treatment Extension Act also made substantial changes in the content of the conservation easement exception in yet a further attempt to clarify the law in this area. The result was to extend the period of uncertainty as to the scope of the conservation easement deduction. This uncertainty is aggravated by the fact that, although Congress charged the Treasury Department to give highest priority to the issuance of regulations pertaining to the conservation easement deduction,[90] and despite the fact that regulations have existed in draft form for quite some time, Treasury has not yet published its proposed regulations.[91] At the present time, the only guide to interpreting the new tax deduction provision is the Congressional committee reports that accompanied it.[92] Consequently, it will take some time to develop any real confidence in dealing with this legislation.

The conservation easement exception to the nondeductibility of gifts of partial interests in real property is termed a "qualified conservation contribution" in the new legislation. In order to qualify, the contribution must be "(A) of a qualified real property interest, (B) to a qualified organization, (C) exclusively for conservation purposes" (§ 170(h)(1)).

A qualified real property interest is defined at Section 170(h)(2) as:

(A) the entire interest of the donor other than a qualified mineral interest [any subsurface minerals may be retained but they may not be removed by surface methods].
(B) a remainder interest, and
(C) a restriction (granted in perpetuity) on the use which may be made of the real property.

Besides adding a fee gift with mineral rights retained to the list of qualified interests, the new definition replaces the former category of leases, options to purchase and easements with the more general category of "restriction (granted in perpetuity)." This change was intended to assure that the local vagaries of real property law not control the availability of the deduction and that easements, as well as other real property interests having similar attributes under state laws, such as restrictive covenants, will qualify.[93] The restrictive effect of the interest granted rather than its formal legal classification is what matters.

Governments and publicly supported charities, along with their subsidiaries, are the only organizations qualified to accept conservation contributions (§ 170(h)(3)). Qualified organizations must have "the commitment and the resources" to enforce the interest created.[94] How this capacity is to be demonstrated is not specified. Presumably, Treasury will be justified in requiring some manner of proof of it, but a special enforcement fund is not required.[95] Congress contemplates that qualified interests, once created, are to be transferable only among qualified organizations.[96]

These first two requirements for the qualified conservation contribution are relatively straightforward.[97] It is the third requirement, the conservation purpose, that will be the real test. The new conservation purpose definition, much expanded from the 1976 version, is at Section 170(h)(4) and reads as follows:

(4) CONSERVATION PURPOSE DEFINED—

(A) IN GENERAL. —For purposes of this subsection, the term "conservation purpose" means—

(i) the preservation of land areas for outdoor recreation by, or for the education of, the general public,

(ii) the protection of a relatively natural habitat of fish, wildlife, or plants, or similar ecosystem,

(iii) the preservation of open space (including farmland and forest land) where such preservation is—

(I) for the scenic enjoyment of the general public, or

(II) pursuant to a clearly delineated Federal, State, or local governmental conservation policy,

and will yield a significant public benefit, or

(iv) the preservation of an historically important land area or a certified historic structure.

As with the 1976 statutory conservation purposes definition, this new conservation purpose test, even though considerably more detailed than its predecessor, vests extensive discretion in the Treasury Department to determine the scope of the deduction. How the conservation purpose test is interpreted will have profound consequences for the future of the easement approach to land conservation. Although it is impossible to predict what Treasury will do, some general observations concerning select aspects of this and certain other policy issues raised by the new qualified conservation contribution deduction may nevertheless prove useful.

The observations that follow rely heavily on the Senate Finance Committee Report that accompanied the 1980 legislation. For a document of its type, the Committee Report is unusually lengthy and detailed in its discussion of the conservation contribution deduction, making it an excellent source for educing the intent of Congress in enacting this legislation. However, the language of the new deduction provision raises many questions that the Committee Report does not answer. Until the Treasury regulations are released or a sufficient number of rulings are obtained—or until further action is taken by Congress—it is impossible to offer anything but the most tentative analysis of the provision. These observations are offered by way of encouraging a thoughtful approach to the issues raised by the federal deduction language. They are not intended to be and should not be regarded as conclusive.

OBSERVATIONS

Public Benefit. Conservation easement law will, for federal income tax purposes, take a fresh start with this newly revised deduction for contributions for conservation purposes. Because the availability of a deduction—at least to those in California for whom Proposition 13 has for the time being brought sufficient property tax relief—may be the principal economic incentive for granting a conservation easement, this new federal legislation is likely to be the key to the success of the conservation easement concept. However, the indication from the legislative history of the Tax Treatment Extension Act is that Treasury will interpret and enforce the new conservation contribution section with great care. Donors and conservation organizations are best advised, at least in the beginning, to proceed with abundant caution.

When legislation to remove the sunset date on the conservation easement deduction was first proposed, Treasury opposed it, believing that the conservation easement deduction had serious potential for abuse. Treasury had two threshold concerns. First, it felt that it was an unnecessary and unjustifiable expenditure of the public's tax dollars to give a deduction for a gift of a conservation easement where the gift would, in many instances, have no material effect on the donor's intended use of the property.[98] A Treasury official likened such gifts to the nondeductible gift to a museum of a remainder interest in a painting: nothing of real current value to the taxpayer is given up.[99] The analogy is not precise; land, unlike a painting, can be developed, and that potential is both independently valuable and immediately severable. Treasury's second concern, however, was more fundamental: there should be a provable benefit to the public if the public is to support conservation easements through the tax laws.[100]

In its final form the 1980 federal tax legislation embodies a compromise between Treasury's desire to forestall potential abuses of the conservation easement device and the desire of conservation organizations to be able to offer a liberal deduction to prospective donors of valuable conservation interests. While expanded to include the full spectrum of open space uses within the scope of the deduction, the new conservation contribution section is designed to insure that a substantial benefit will accrue to the public from the donation of a qualified interest. As the Committee Report states:

The Committee believes that provisions allowing deductions for conservation easements should be directed at the preservation of unique or otherwise significant land areas or structures. The Committee bill would restrict the qualifying contributions where there is no assurance that the public benefit, if any, furthered by the contribution would be substantial enough to justify the allowance of a deduction.[101]

The Act seeks to accomplish this in two ways. First, for tax deduction purposes, only governmental entities and publicly supported charities are qualified to accept these interests; private foundations are excluded. Public purpose and public accountability are, presumably, inherent in this requirement. Second, the definition of "conservation purpose," both by its terms and as expounded in the Committee Report, is intended to restrict the allowance of a deduction in such a way that only those interests that produce a public benefit will qualify. Stating the public benefit requirement, however, is much easier than determining what interests meet it. There is likely to be much room for interpretation and, depending on how narrowly Treasury chooses to define public benefit, much room for dispute.

As a preliminary matter, the Committee Report makes it clear that a conservation easement, to be deductible, need meet the requirements of only one of the four categories of qualified conservation purposes.[102] However, a deduction will not be accorded an easement that advances one qualified conservation purpose at the expense of another.[103] If under the terms of an otherwise qualifying farmland easement, to use the example given by the Committee Report, the use of pesticides is permitted and that use might "significantly" injure a natural ecosystem, no deduction will be allowed.[104] Assuming that a given conservation contribution protective of one set of conservation values is not destructive of other significant conservation values, a determination must then be made as to whether the public benefit derived from the contribution is substantial enough to justify the allowance of a deduction for it.

Subsections (i) and (iv): Public Recreation, Education and Historic Land Areas and Structures. The public benefit to be derived from lands restricted for outdoor recreation by, and education of, the general public under subsection (i) of the conservation purpose definition should be clear enough in all cases where real opportunity for use by the public at large is present and the lands in question are, in fact, suited to and attractive of public use. Likewise, public benefit flowing from the preservation of certified historic structures under subsection (iv) is presumably assured by the cooperative state–federal certification process. There is likely to be less certainty with respect to historic land areas for which no certification is obtained. The Committee Report speaks of "independently significant land areas" and gives, as an example, a civil war battlefield.[105] Many historic sites should easily qualify for deductibility. What criteria will be applied to determine the "significance" of a given site in marginal cases, however, remains to be seen.

Subsection (ii): Relatively Natural Habitat or Ecosystem. Satisfying the public benefit requirement of subsection (ii)—the protection of a "relatively natural habitat"—will be more problematic than satisfying subsection (i). Subsection (ii) seems rather unrestrictive on the face of it. "Relatively natural habitat" can, under certain circumstances, mean such man-altered habitats as dammed lakes or salt ponds that are used as feeding areas by wildlife.[106] However, the fact that an area is relatively natural and provides habitat for wildlife is not sufficient to qualify it under subsection (ii). The area to be protected by the easement must also be, in some demonstrable way, ecologically important. Only "significant habitats and ecosystems" will yield the necessary public benefit to qualify under subsection (ii).[107] A natural area will be considered significant if rare, endangered or threatened species are present, or if it is within or contributes to the ecological viability of a park or other conservation area, or otherwise represents a "high quality" native terrestrial or aquatic ecosystem.[108]

Testing the limits of this natural ecosystem preservation purpose will likely produce considerable dispute at the margin, and the "high quality" criteria contained in the Committee Report signal caution. Latitude is given the IRS to interpret this category broadly or narrowly, and, if Treasury's early opposition to the Dingell bill is any indication, a narrow interpretation is most likely. Persons seeking to qualify the grant of an easement under subsection (ii) should, as a basis for proving the significance of the contribution, make every effort to document the resource values of the land in question with care and precision. The circumstances may even call for a thorough professional environmental assessment report analyzing the important ecological characteristics of the land and including such relevant supporting documentation as photographs and maps relating to soil types, water sources and quality, geological features, vegetation and significant wildlife species. A claim of ecological significance is likely to be subjected to close scrutiny by the IRS. Conservation organizations and their contributors should be prepared to meet it up front.

Subsection (iii): Open Space Lands. If an easement cannot meet the significance test of subsection (ii), there remains the catchall category of subsection (iii). Its requirements are likely to be applicable to by far the largest number of conservation easements. Subsection (iii) poses thorny definitional problems. Since there was no equivalent of subsection (iii) in the 1976 amendment, conservation organizations continued to look to the "undivided interest" exception as the basis for the most common types of conservation easement grants. When in the course of debate over the Dingell bill it became apparent that the new legislation would supersede the undivided interest exception with respect to conservation easements,[109] conservation organizations lobbied for a category that would include typical farmland, wetland and forest land easements. Subsection (iii) is the result. It is significant as the first expressly codified recognition by Congress that the protection of farm, forest and other such open space represents a qualified charitable activity. However, there is likely to be much controversy over its intended scope. Again, the IRS is left with broad discretion to determine what kinds of easements qualify.

SCENIC. A scenic easement must be for "the scenic enjoyment of the general public." As the Committee Report states, "Visual, not physical, access by the general public to the property is sufficient."[110] However, whether a scenic easement will be sanctioned only if the entire area under restriction is visible from a public place is unclear. It can be argued that where development of nonvisible portions of a property will adversely impact the visible scenic portions of that property or lead to the degradation of a larger viewshed of which the property is a part, a deduction for a scenic easement over nonvisible scenic lands should be allowed. The integral nature of visible and nonvisible portions of scenic properties and areas should be taken into account. Similarly, protection of nonscenic land whose development would adversely affect neighboring scenic lands should also be considered to be for scenic enjoyment. An example might be a scenic easement over ordinary farmland to protect the view from a public highway of a nearby mountain range. The Committee Report could be read to support either a broad or narrow interpretation of what qualifies as a deductible scenic easement. It states only that preservation of land may be determined to be for the scenic enjoyment of the general public if "development of the property would interfere with a scenic panorama that can be enjoyed" from a place that is open to the public.[111] How direct such interference must be to meet the scenic enjoyment test is not specified.

NONSCENIC. The test for deductibility of a nonscenic open space easement is perhaps the most vague and troublesome of all. What is meant by "pursuant to a clearly delineated Federal, State or local governmental conservation policy" is not immediately apparent, and the Committee Report does not shed much additional light on the question. In the first place, the phrase "pursuant to" a governmental policy could be construed to mean that an easement would have to be granted to or approved by a governmental entity. Consistency with the policy, at this stage, might not be enough. Second, what constitutes a "clearly delineated governmental policy" is far from clear. Interestingly, although the word "policy" is used in the statute, the words "program" and "project" appear in the Committee Report.[112] This is indicative of a preference for the specific over the general, but just how focused a project must be on specific land areas individually identified for conservation uses is not clear. The Report states that the statute does not require that a program be funded, but it must represent a "significant commitment by the government."[113] How that commitment is to be expressed is not stated, but the Report does indicate that broad declarations of governmental policy by state legislatures are inadequate.[114]

There are numerous governmental projects at all levels of government in California that should be able to meet the "clearly delineated governmental policy" test, and any funded program is almost certain to qualify. The Coastal Act, the wild and scenic rivers program and programs for the protection of San Francisco Bay and Suisun Marsh come readily to mind, but there are many other local and regional park and open space programs that manifest a significant governmental commitment to conservation. However, many of these programs involve scenic or recreation areas that would qualify, in any case, under the tests for scenic or recreation easements. Until government, particularly local government, becomes more active in this field, many nonscenic easements will have no program to which to attach themselves, unless recourse is had to the Open-Space Easement Act.

Consequently, whether an easement granted under the Open-Space Easement Act represents a sufficiently specific expression of governmental conservation policy becomes an important question. If it does, the Open-Space Easement Act may take on renewed significance in light of the new federal deduction language. If it does not, the use of nonscenic open space easements as a land preservation tool in California may be limited, at least in the near future, for lack of a more clearly delineated governmental policy concerning nonscenic open space protection. However, because an easement granted under the Open-Space Easement Act must conform to a local government's state-mandated and state-approved open space plan, because a specific finding must be made in every case that a particular easement is in the public interest and serves local conservation or open space values and because the local government in whose jurisdiction an open space easement is situated must itself either accept or approve the easement, it would seem that easements granted under the Open-Space Easement Act should meet the "clearly delineated governmental policy" test. The entire process is so clearly focused on the individual easement in question that it would be difficult for the IRS to deny that, however general the statewide program might be, the easement was granted and accepted pursuant to a clearly delineated *local* governmental conservation policy.

SIGNIFICANT PUBLIC BENEFIT. Proving that an easement has a qualified purpose under subsection (iii) does not end with the showing that it is either for the scenic enjoyment of the general public or pursuant to a clearly delineated governmental conservation policy. Although the Committee Report indicates that the entire conservation interest deduction section was drafted as it was to insure that the public benefit flowing from an easement gift would be substantial enough to justify the tax incentive proffered for it,[115] subsection (iii) includes an express public benefit provision. Gifts under subsection (iii), after meeting the threshold scenic enjoyment or governmental policy test, must be shown to "yield a significant public benefit" as well. According to the Committee Report, all information concerning an easement gift will be evaluated to determine the public benefit of the gift.[116]

Considerations the Committee Report indicated might enter into a determination of public benefit include: (1) uniqueness of the property, (2) intensity of existing and foreseeable development in the vicinity, (3) consistency of the proposed open space use with federal, state or local programs for conservation in the region and (4) opportunity for public use or appreciation of the restricted land.[117] The types of governmental programs that might satisfy the consistency test for public benefit are "water supply protection, water quality maintenance or enhancement, flood prevention and control, erosion control, shoreline protection, and protection of land areas included in, or related to, a government approved master plan or land management area."[118] Although neither the four enumerated public benefit factors, nor the governmental programs used to illustrate the consistency factor, should be considered exhaustive, they do provide a strong indication of what Congress considers important in evaluating scenic and open space easements. The relevancy of the factors will vary, and other factors may prove decisive in a given case, but every subsection (iii) easement must exhibit some distinctive public purpose.

Whatever it may add to scenic easements, the significant public benefit requirement would appear to be redundant when applied to open space easements that have already met the clearly delineated governmental conservation policy test. Presumably, the creation of a public benefit is the intended purpose of any governmental program and is therefore implied in the clearly delineated governmental policy requirement. However, the express public benefit test may be an indication that the protection of nonscenic farm and forest land for its own sake, however clearly sanctioned by governmental policy, is not yet recognized as a sufficient conservation purpose under the open space deduction, and some additional element of singularity or some parallel conservation program (such as water quality control) must be evoked to qualify the easement.

The Committee Report gives as an example of a qualifying open space easement the preservation of farmland pursuant to a state program for flood prevention control.[119] Mention of state or local programs for farm or forest land preservation is conspicuously absent. One could conclude from this that if the easement were given, to take the Committee Report's example, pursuant to a flood control program in the first instance, then the significant public benefit test would be redundant. However, if the easement were given pursuant to a state program for farmland protection, it is possible that consistency with some additional governmental program, such as flood control, would have to be shown. Such a reading of the statute may be an exceedingly narrow one, but it does find some support in the Committee Report. A growing awareness of the threat to the nation's wealth represented by the accelerating conversion of farm and forest land to other uses may, however, make the possibility of its assertion increasingly more remote.

If the significant public benefit test is applied to easements granted under the Open-Space Easement Act—assuming open space easements are found to satisfy the clearly delineated governmental policy test—such easements should meet it easily. Easements granted under the Open-Space Easement Act must be consistent with local open space and general plans. That requirement makes it certain that they will be "included in, or related to, a government approved master plan," thereby satisfying the consistency factor suggested by the Committee Report as an indicator of public benefit.

The public benefit test under subsection (iii), as expounded by the Committee Report, is undoubtedly intended to operate as a check on open space easements. In a sense, the test adds nothing new. All contributions for conservation purposes must yield a public benefit, and the factors that the Committee Report lists as productive of public benefit for open space easements under subsection (iii) will certainly be relevant to recreational or natural habitat easements as well. However, it is with open space easements that there is perceived to be the most room for abuse. This is likely to be both the most frequently used category and the category in which the most borderline cases are presented. The express public benefit test provides the IRS with a tool—however vague or redundant it may appear to be—for scrutinizing those donations that give less to the public good than they would take back in the form of a tax deduction.

Valuation. Appraising the value of a conservation easement donation is a crucial step in the process of entering into a conservation easement transaction. However, until a market for conservation easements develops or until a substantial history of sales of restricted properties is available, valuation of conservation easements will be a difficult and imprecise science. Concern that this imprecision could lead to abusive or so-called aggressive valuations that would be difficult to police was a substantial motivating factor in Treasury's early opposition to making the conservation easement deduction permanent.[120]

The method sanctioned by Congress for valuing conservation easements takes an indirect approach because of the lack in the usual case of market evidence of the value of such interests.[121] Called the "before-and-after" method, and approved by Treasury since 1973, this approach attempts to ascertain the fair market value of an easement by measuring "the difference between the fair market value of the total property before the granting of the easement and the fair market value of the property after the grant."[122] In the usual case, the restrictions on development imposed by a conservation easement will reduce the market value of the burdened property, and the amount by which the value of the property is reduced is the amount that the donor can claim as a deduction.

The goal of the before-and-after method is to isolate that portion of the market value of a property attributable to its development potential by examining such data as location, local growth patterns, the availability of utilities, access, topography, taxes, existing land use restrictions and the like.[123] In analyzing these factors, all the usual tools of the appraiser will come into play. If the subject property has not changed hands recently, market data on properties with similar characteristics will provide a useful indicator of value. The sale prices of comparable properties in close proximity to the subject property can be analyzed for evidence of "before" value, and the sale prices of comparable properties situated in areas with little or no development pressure can be examined for evidence of "after" value. In addition, the value of any improvements and the income potential of the property can be factored in, if significant. However, because of the multiplicity of factors involved and the high degree of subjectivity that will necessarily enter into their analysis, it is likely to be some time before "after" values can be appraised with any completely reliable degree of accuracy.

The Committee Report offers some advice on valuation. Factors to be considered are not only the current use of the property but the likelihood of development absent the conservation contribution.[124] Applicable zoning and other existing governmental restrictions on development of the property should be factored in.[125] The impact of an easement on the value of a taxpayer's adjacent property (in some cases there will be an increase in the value of adjacent lands because of the assured amenity of neighboring open space) should be taken into account.[126] In the case of an easement given on a partial parcel, the effect of the donation on the overall value of the property rather

59

than merely the restricted portion is what matters.[127] Of course, where an easement enhances rather than decreases the market value of the property in question (the example is given of the premium that may attach to certain historic properties), no deduction will be allowed.[128]

A proportionate part of a donor's cost basis in his property will be attributed to an easement gift.[129] The percentage of the fair market value of the entire property that the easement represents is the percentage by which the donor's basis will be reduced.[130] Gain upon a subsequent sale of the property will be adjusted accordingly.

The IRS closely scrutinizes donation valuations. Donors of easements claiming substantial deductions should anticipate challenges from the IRS on the issue of value. It is advisable to choose appraisers for their independence and credibility rather than their liberality. Every effort should be made to achieve accuracy, and the process should be well documented. It should be noted that the cost of appraisals made in connection with the donation of an easement or any gift of land is deductible as an expense incurred by a taxpayer in determining his income tax liability under Section 212(3) of the Internal Revenue Code.[131]

Perpetuity. A central requirement for a qualifying conservation interest is that it be granted in perpetuity and that the conservation purposes for which it was granted be protected in perpetuity. This requirement embodies what is meant by a qualified deduction made *"exclusively* for conservation purposes" (I.R.C. § 170(h)(5)(A) [emphasis added]). The requirement begs a number of the same questions that are left unanswered in the California Conservation Easements Act. These questions cluster around the possibility of abandonment by the donee through dissolution or failure to enforce, as well as the possibility that changed circumstances might make the restriction obsolete.

For tax purposes, the established rule is that if, at the time a gift is made, the possibility that it might be negated by some future event appears "so remote as to be negligible," a deduction will be allowed.[132] Once the statute of limitations has run with respect to a given year's return, an easement deduction cannot be attacked for lack of perpetuity or on any other ground. However, the regulations to be issued by Treasury are likely to require that certain assurances of perpetuity be evidenced at the time a gift is made. The Committee

Report makes it clear that "the contribution must involve legally enforceable restrictions on the interest in the property retained by the donor that would prevent uses of the retained interest inconsistent with the conservation purposes."[133] These restrictions should be recorded and must be enforceable against not only the donor but against any subsequent owner of the property in question.[134] Conservation easements granted pursuant to the California Conservation Easements Act will, by their nature, satisfy the requirement that the donor's interest be perpetually restricted, as will restrictive covenants in the case of a fee gift (less mineral rights) or a remainder interest.

With respect to the interest granted to the donee, the Committee Report goes on to state the following:

> The requirement that the conservation purpose be protected in perpetuity also is intended to limit deductible contributions to those transfers which require that the donee (or successor in interest) hold the conservation easement (or other restriction) or other property interests exclusively for conservation purposes (i.e., that they not be transferable by the donee except to other qualified organizations that also will hold the perpetual restriction or property exclusively for conservation purposes).[135]

Again, for a California conservation easement, this requirement poses no problems. The California Conservation Easements Act requires virtually the same thing. The question of how a donee's fee interest (less mineral rights) or remainder interest should be restricted, however, does create an interesting problem.

Presumably, the only way the donee's interest in the gift of a fee (less mineral rights) or a remainder interest could be enforceably restricted would be by the insertion of restrictions in the deed to the donee or by the grant of a conservation easement over the same property to a second qualified organization. The latter method would prove cumbersome, even if, which is unlikely, an organization could be found that would be willing to hold such an interest. In any case, requiring one qualified organization to hold a conservation easement over property owned by another would result in a wasteful misallocation of resources that could not be said to be within the contemplation of the new conservation contribution section of the Code. Requiring deed restrictions to be enforced by the grantor, on the other hand, while certain to have the effect of clouding title, would do little to assure the perpetuity of the original conservation purpose of the grant, particularly after the motivated grantor is gone from the scene. Even if such a restriction were created in favor of a conservation organization, assuming one were willing to accept it, there would still be no guarantee that that organization would want to maintain the property for the original conservation purpose any more than the original donee.

In short, there really is no way effectively to guarantee the perpetuation of the original conservation use of a fee interest once it is in the hands of a qualified donee, and there is little to be gained from trying. After all, it is the donee organization itself that will be in the best position to know the most beneficial use of the property in light of its public charitable goals. The conservation values of a donated parcel may diminish in time or may prove inferior to those of another parcel whose purchase could be funded by the sale of the donated parcel. As long as it remains faithful to its charter purposes, a qualified donee ought to be free to respond as it sees fit to any change in conditions affecting property it owns outright. The only really effective safeguard of the conservation purpose of such gifts is the integrity of the original qualified donee. If a qualified organization, shown to possess the requisite commitment and resources, can be relied on to protect the conservation purpose of a grant against its grantor, it should be trusted to protect those same purposes as the owner of the property in question.

There will be occasions when a donor, for his own reasons, wishes to insure that an outright fee or remainder gift is used in perpetuity for a conservation purpose. Carefully drafted deed restrictions are appropriate under such circumstances. To insure the long-range enforceability of such restrictions, and to assure that the full market value of the property can be used for the deduction, it is advisable that the reversionary interest be given to a third party who is also a qualified donee. A similar device might be useful for a gift of a conservation easement as well. Providing that the easement interest will pass to a second qualified donee under specified conditions can protect against any material diminution of the primary donee's ability to enforce the easement, including abandonment resulting from the dissolution of the primary donee organization. One commentator suggests that a clause assigning the donor's reversionary rights to a qualified third party (either predetermined or to be named by a court) may even be necessary to provide the "reasonable assurance" of perpetuity the IRS requires to sanction the deductibility of an easement gift.[136] For governmental entities and many nonprofit organizations with proven track records, reasonable assurance of perpetuity exists without resort to provision for a substitute grantee. For the newer land trusts and other unproven nonprofit organizations, however, the executory limitation clause could provide a useful backup.

Relation to the California Open-Space and Conservation Easements Acts. The California Conservation Easements Act and the Open-Space Easement Act are not coextensive with the federal tax deduction legislation. Easements that might qualify under either or both of the California acts may not qualify for a federal tax deduction, and, conversely, easements that might otherwise qualify for a federal tax deduction may not fit either the conservation or open space easement legislation.

Qualified Purpose and Qualified Donee. Both the Conservation Easements Act and the federal deduction section allow wide latitude as to the form a conservation restriction may take, but the Conservation Easements Act is broader than the federal conservation contribution deduction with respect to its purposes. The Conservation Easements Act was intended to be comprehensive; it encompasses virtually any imaginable open space or conservation purpose and, unlike the federal legislation, imposes no elaborate qualifying tests. However, to obtain federal and state tax deductions for a conservation easement, a donor must meet the stricter qualifying requirements of the federal deduction section. In structuring a conservation easement, the donor's focus must be on the federal tests. Compliance with the terms of the Open-Space Easement Act, by contrast, may by itself provide at least a very strong argument that the qualifying purpose requirements of the federal deduction section have been met.

The federal deduction section is at once broader and narrower than the Open-Space Easement Act and the Conservation Easements Act with respect to the definition of a qualified organization. Under the Open-Space Easement Act, local governments and all organizations qualified under 501(c)(3) of the Internal Revenue Code as tax-exempt organizations may acquire open space easements so long as they include the preservation of open space as a stated purpose in their articles of incorporation (Gov't Code § 51075(f)). Qualification

63

must be demonstrated by a letter of determination from the IRS. Under the Conservation Easements Act, state and local governmental entities and 501(c)(3) organizations qualified to do business in California whose "primary purpose" is land preservation may acquire and hold conservation easements (§ 815.3). For its part, the federal deduction requires that a qualified holder be a governmental unit, a publicly supported charity or a subsidiary of either of these (I.R.C. § 170(h)(3)). Private foundations, eligible as easement recipients under the broad acceptance by both California laws of all 501(c)(3) organizations, are *not* qualified organizations for purposes of federal tax deductibility. On the other hand, to qualify under federal tax law, a nonprofit organization need not have an express conservation or open space purpose. A donor will receive a deduction for a qualified contribution to any publicly supported charity regardless of the organization's stated purposes. However, in California, a qualified organization lacking the requisite charter purpose must take care only to accept those interests it is sure it can enforce under the common law.

Differences in the breadth of purpose and the definition of qualified holders between the California easement legislation and the federal deduction section are important but should create no problem for the donation of easements of genuine public value so long as the parties involved are aware of them and structure their transactions so as to qualify under both the applicable state and federal legislation. Gifts of Section 815 conservation easements will be deductible if the federal requirements are met; there is no unavoidable conflict between the two. However, open space easements under the Open-Space Easement Act, because of certain provisions of that Act, could conceivably encounter difficulties relating to deductibility. The problematic provisions of the Open-Space Easement Act are those concerning property tax relief, abandonment and the effect of condemnation proceedings on an easement.

Property Tax Relief: A Quid Pro Quo? The purpose of the Open-Space Easement Act was and still is to protect open space lands from rapidly encroaching development. Its method is to offer, as an inducement, automatic property tax relief to those landowners who participate in the program. It has been suggested that the property tax relief made available by legislation of this type might be viewed as the equivalent of consideration, which, if it were so, would transform the gift of an open space easement into a nondeductible *quid pro quo* transaction.[137]

A charitable easement gift must be gratuitous in order to be deductible; a taxpayer's dominant motivation in making it cannot be the expectation of some economic benefit (ignoring, of course, the degree to which the deduction itself may be a motivating factor).[138] Incidental benefit to the taxpayer, however, if outweighed by the benefit accruing to the public from the gift, will not result in loss of a deduction.[139] The usual nondeductible situation is presented by the case where an easement or dedication is given in a direct exchange for favorable zoning or development approval.[140] In virtually every reported case where a deduction has been denied, the taxpayer received an economic benefit from the governmental entity involved that was direct, immediate and, most important, bargained for.[141]

The property tax relief available under the Open-Space Easement Act, on the other hand, is statutorily imposed; no bargaining element is involved. The fact that the Open-Space Easement Act makes property tax relief available automatically may, depending on the property tax burden of a given donor, have little or nothing to do with a decision to grant an easement under its terms. In fact, the Open-Space Easement Act's history of disuse would indicate that the availability of automatic property tax relief has not been an important motivating factor in decisions to donate conservation easements. Lowered property taxes should result from most conservation easement donations in any case, as a reflection of the loss of that element of market value represented by development potential—at least to the extent such value has not already escaped taxation because of Proposition 13. The income capitalization method that is applicable to open space easements under the Open-Space Easement Act may, but need not, result in a lower assessed value for restricted properties than other methods. Except for those few cases where an easement gift does not decrease the market value of the property, there ought to be no significant difference between the property tax relief available under the Open-Space Easement Act and that which would follow from a donation made outside the terms of the Act. In those cases where market value is not reduced, of course, there would be no loss in value on which to base a deduction in any event.

To view the property tax relief offered by the Open-Space Easement Act as the dominant motive for the grant of a perpetual open space easement would be to miss the point that a perpetual grant is unnecessary to obtain property tax relief under the Act—an easement for a term of ten years, renewable annually, would suffice. In addition, an easement need not be donated; the property tax relief offered by the Act applies equally to the sale of an open space easement as to a gift. In a perpetual grant by donation under the Open-Space Easement Act, a broader motive than the desire to reduce property taxes must be at work. The automatic property tax relief scheme of the Open-Space Easement Act ought to serve as good evidence of the significance of a local government's commitment to the open space policy advanced by the Act. To treat it as fair consideration for a perpetual easement grant, however, is to assign it weightier significance than it deserves.

Abandonment. The two other provisions that may affect the deductibility of an open space easement granted in accordance with the Open-Space Easement Act trench upon the perpetuity requirement of the federal legislation. Section 51093 of the Act provides a means by which a landowner may petition for abandonment of an open space easement that has become unduly burdensome. Here, as throughout much of the Act, the focus would appear logically to be on term easements under which the landowner has retained an explicit reversionary interest and, in effect, seeks acceleration of that interest. In fact, Section 51090 expressly states that the Act's provisions for termination are exclusive for term easements. However, no separate mention is made of perpetual easements, and Section 51093 could be interpreted to permit abandonment of a perpetual easement at the initiation of the landowner, inconsistent as that might be with the concept of a perpetual grant. The decision to abandon rests squarely with the governmental body, however, and must be based on a finding that no public purpose remains for keeping the land as open space—a high threshold, which, if honestly applied, should be no less stringent than the standard a court might apply in determining the continuing viability of any conservation easement.

If conservation and open space easements are to be realistic real property mechanisms, some means must be available for their adaptation to change. The right to petition for abandonment and the procedures triggered by such a petition under Section 51093 could be seen as an effort to accommodate this need in a straightforward but strictly controlled manner. Viewed in this light, the availability of an abandonment procedure should be no cause for calling into question the perpetual nature of an easement gift. The possibility that abandonment might occur would be no greater than for an easement made outside the Act: "so remote as to be negligible."[142] As the California Supreme Court held with respect to the analogous but significantly less restrictive Williamson Act cancellation provision, only "extraordinary circumstances" could ever justify abandonment.[143] However, the IRS may take a different view, reasoning that, to the extent the abandonment procedure resembles the zoning process, viable easements will be subject to political whim. To avoid the consequences of such an interpretation, a landowner might wish to consider making an express waiver of the abandonment petition privilege. By so doing he would leave the question of termination of an open space easement to the determination of the courts, where, presumably, it would lie for any other perpetual restriction, deductible or not, that has outlived its social usefulness.

Condemnation. Finally, Section 51095 of the Open-Space Easement Act provides that a donated open space easement shall terminate upon the filing of a complaint in condemnation against property that has been restricted by it. Again, this provision calls into question the perpetual nature of the gift and opens up the possibility that a deduction might be given for the donation of property rights for which, at a later date, a landowner might also receive fair market value. This provision may give the IRS pause. Its purpose is clear enough: it protects open space land, whether restricted in perpetuity or for a term of years, from becoming an easy target for eminent domain. Without such a provision, the open space easement program for the protection of open space could be defeated. Not only would landowners be discouraged from participating by the threat of becoming easy marks for condemnation, but the land preservation purpose of the Act could be compromised by a governmental entity's too facile conversion of open space land to other more intensive uses. Section 51095 prevents the Open-Space Easement Act from becoming at once both a trap for landowners and an ineffective and self-defeating open space protection tool.

Again, the position of the Treasury Department is that where the possibility that an interest in property donated to a charity can be defeated by some future occurrence is so remote as to be negligible, the value of the gift is deductible.[144] The same reasoning may be applicable to the possibility of termination of an easement in the event of condemnation, and at least one private ruling has been obtained to this effect.[145] A strong argument can be made not only that the possibility of condemnation occurring on land subject to an open space easement is negligible, but that Section 51095, by keeping governmental agencies honest, was intended to insure that it be negligible.

It should be noted that the donor of an easement will not receive a windfall if an easement for which a deduction was allowed is later terminated or abandoned. If the donor is still the owner of the property, the previously deducted value of the easement now restored will be taxed to him under the so-called tax benefit rule. Succinctly stated, this rule requires that if an "amount deducted from income in one taxable year is recovered in a later year, the recovery is income in the later year."[146] However, whether the recovered value of the easement gift would be recognized as income in the year the easement is extinguished or only later, when the property is sold and payment is received for it, is not clear.[147]

Private nonprofit organizations were given a role in the Open-Space Easement Act in anticipation that they would be able to "sell" the idea to landowners in a way that local governments had not. The federal tax deduction is the strongest economic selling point these organizations have. If perpetual easements granted under the Open-Space Easement Act were determined to be nondeductible, the Open-Space Easement Act would, for most purposes, become a dead letter.

Administrative Matters. Many potential donors and donees of conservation easements and other interests in real property affected by the 1980 changes in the federal tax law dealing with conservation contributions are holding back from granting and accepting conservation easements because Treasury's interpretive regulations have yet to be published. People are uncertain of the scope of Section 170(h), and the risks are such that very few can afford to act without first knowing that their gifts will qualify. It is apparent that "the whole key to this program is certainty."[148] To this end, not only did Congress elevate the drafting of regulations for this section to priority status, it also stated that taxpayers should be able to obtain prior administrative determinations concerning qualification even before the issuance of the regulations.[149] Although engaging the private letter ruling process can be expensive, in the absence of regulations, persons wishing to complete easement donations should seek rulings in all cases where there exists a significant possibility of challenge.

Federal interest in conservation easements and other less-than-fee alternatives to outright acquisition of sensitive lands is surging in the atmosphere of fiscal constraint that has descended on Washington.[150] Careful attention will be paid to the workings of the conservation easement deduction. Bemoaning the lack of a comprehensive data base for evaluating the provisions relating to conservation contributions, the Committee Report ends by requesting that Treasury undertake a study of conservation interests for submission to Congress by 1985.[151] Only by closely monitoring deductions claimed for conservation contributions will Treasury be able to meet this charge.

Wild and Scenic Rivers Act. The existence, in one context, of an interesting penalty to encourage compliance by a donor with the terms of a conservation easement should be noted. The allowance of a deduction for the donation of a conservation easement on property located within a federally designated wild and scenic river area obligates the donor to perform its terms or be subject to the right of the donee or the United States to acquire the entire property for its fair market value, minus easement value, as of the time the easement was donated.[152]

Federal Estate and Gift Tax
(I.R.C. §§ 2055(e)(2), 2106(a)(2)(e) and 2522(c)(2); § 2032A)

Deductions are allowed for federal estate and gift tax purposes for donations and bequests of qualified conservation contributions as defined by Section 170(h) pertaining to the income tax deduction. Formerly, estate taxes on the value of real property represented a heavy burden for many landowners, often necessitating the sale and premature development of lands that surviving families might otherwise have maintained in an open space condition. Consequently, reduction of estate taxes was an important, sometimes critical, incentive for the donation of partial interests in real property, whether made *inter vivos* or by will. In the case of donors in very high tax brackets, the avoidance of estate taxes in conjunction with an income tax deduction could even result in the recovery through tax savings of the entire value of the donated interest.[153] For others, the added savings of estate taxes was, if not so dramatic, nevertheless significant.

The Economic Recovery Tax Act of 1981 (ERTA)[154] brought changes to the federal estate and gift tax law that have reduced the significance of federal estate taxes for the donation of a conservation easement. Under ERTA, the maximum tax rate is to be reduced from 70 to 50 percent over a five-year period, while at the same time the unified credit is to be increased from $62,800 to $192,800, thereby raising the estate tax exemption from $225,000 to $600,000. By the time the $600,000 exemption is fully phased in, federal estate taxes will, reportedly, remain a factor for only approximately one-half of one percent of the U.S. population.[155] Included in this small percentage, however, will be many large farm and ranch operators in California for whom the effect of an easement donation on estate taxes will continue to be of great consequence.

Section 2032A of the Internal Revenue Code provides for use valuation, for estate tax purposes, of certain family farm or timberland that will continue to be used by surviving families as farm or timberland. Section 2032A use valuation can produce a substantial reduction in the valuation of property for estate tax purposes—as much as 35 to 60 percent.[156] However, qualification for use valuation is dependent on meeting certain complex requirements and is unnecessary when an easement donation has already been made effectively reducing the market value of a farm property to its use value. Nonetheless, the section could be important for persons who have restricted their property for only a term of years under the Open-Space Easement Act or the Williamson Act.

A word of caution regarding gift taxes: when an *inter vivos* gift of a conservation easement or other partial interest fails to meet the tests for deductibility under Section 170(h), the gift may be subject to a gift tax.[157] The risk of exposure to such tax liability counsels that great care be taken in meeting the tests for deductibility. Theoretically, gift tax liability might also attach to an open space easement granted under the Open-Space Easement Act for a term of years rather than in perpetuity. Even though functionally equivalent to a Williamson Act contract, a term open space easement, if structured as an interest in real property rather than a contractual right (the Open-Space Easement Act, it seems, could be used to create either), falls within the category of nondeductible gifts of partial interests in property. If tested, the grantor of a term easement might prevail with the argument that no gift was intended and that, on the contrary, unlike the donor of a perpetual easement, his overriding motive was the reduction in property taxes that the Open-Space Easement Act affords.

Capital Gains Tax

The gift of a conservation easement not only produces income and estate tax deductions but also avoids capital gains tax on the appreciation applicable to the donated interest. The result is that capital gain is realized in the deduction without being taxed. The basis of the entire property is allocated proportionately to the interest retained and the donated rights, and the amount in excess of the basis applied to the donated rights is the amount of capital gains for which taxation is avoided.[158] If a landowner sells his property in the future, he will pay tax on the gain realized from the sale over that portion of the basis allocated to his retained interest.

STATE TAX LAW

California Income Tax (Rev. & Tax. Code §§ 17214.2, 17214.7, 24357.2 and 24357.7)

Legislation passed in 1982 amended the California Revenue and Taxation Code to conform to federal tax law with respect to qualified conservation contributions.[159] Revenue and Taxation Code Sections 17214.2 and 17214.7 (for individuals) and Sections 24357.2 and 24357.7 (for banks and corporations) are identical to Sections 170(f)(3) and 170(h) of the Internal Revenue Code. The California provisions are applicable to contributions made on or after January 1, 1982 (§§ 17214.2(d) and 24357.2(d)).

California Inheritance Tax (Rev. & Tax. Code §§ 13957, 13841 and 13842); Open Space Land Dedication, 1978 (Gov't Code §§ 7301-7309)

At the primary election on June 8, 1982, the people of California, by approving Propositions 5 and 6 (Rev. & Tax. Code §§ 13301–13304), abolished California inheritance and gift taxes. At the same time, the electorate reenacted a "pick-up" tax that had previously been imposed on estates for which no inheritance tax, or an inheritance tax less than the maximum state death tax credit allowed by the federal estate tax law, was due (former §§ 13441–13443). This "pick-up" tax, equal to the maximum allowable state death tax credit, allows the state to profit from the state tax credit provided by federal law without increasing the tax liability of California estates, since the amount in question would be payable to the United States if no state death tax existed. As a result of the repeal of the California inheritance tax law, such taxes are no longer a factor in decision-making regarding the effect of transfers of conservation easements on estates of persons dying on or after June 8, 1982. With regard to estates of persons who died before that date, the provisions discussed below are still meaningful.

When applicable, California Revenue and Taxation Code Section 13957 provides that real property valued on a use-related basis under Revenue and Taxation Code Sections 423 or 423.5 for property tax purposes shall, at the request of the administrator of an estate, be so valued for inheritance tax purposes unless there are at least five sales of comparable land with comparable enforceable restrictions from which to determine market value. Property restricted under either the Williamson Act or the Open-Space Easement Act can benefit from this provision. As for property restricted by a conservation easement under Civil Code Section 815, that property will, to the extent the easement reduces its market value, be subject to a proportionately smaller inheritance tax liability.

Revenue and Taxation Code Sections 13841 and 13842 provide that government and qualified nonprofit beneficiaries are exempt from inheritance tax.

Prior to repeal of the inheritance tax, Government Code Sections 7301–7309 provided a means of reducing the burden of inheritance taxes on persons, such as family farmers, who were land rich but cash poor, that directly encouraged the preservation of open space lands. Under those sections a person who received an inheritance that did not include sufficient liquid assets to pay the state inheritance tax thereon could offer the state from among the property received "any right or interest, including development rights, in real property which is essentially unimproved and devoted to an open space use as defined in Section 65560 or real property which is of significant historic or cultural value" (§ 7301(a)). If the Secretary of the State Resources Agency, with the approval of the Director of the State Department of Finance, found it feasible to accept the interest, its appraised value, as certified by the inheritance tax referee, would be credited toward the tax due,[160] and the land involved would be "maintained and preserved in perpetuity as open space land" (§ 7307). Because this option to dedicate lands for open space was linked by its terms to the inheritance tax law (§ 7301(b)), the repeal of the inheritance law would appear to have rendered it inoperative with respect to estates opened after June 8, 1982. It is doubtful that an open space dedication would be accepted in lieu of the "pick-up" estate tax.[161]

California Property Tax

OPEN SPACE PROPERTY TAX ASSESSMENT
(REV. & TAX. CODE §§ 421–430.5)

Sections 421–430.5 of the Revenue and Taxation Code govern the valuation of open space lands subject to certain enforceable restrictions. These sections, adopted under the authority of Article XXVIII (now Article XIII, Section 8) of the California Constitution, provide for the assessment of open space lands on a use-related rather than full-cash-value basis. They are at the heart of the California legislature's original design for open space protection. The property tax relief embodied in Sections 421–430.5 was intended to supply an incentive both for the grant of easements under the Open-Space Easement Act and the use of Williamson Act contracts.

Williamson Act contracts and agreements, wildlife habitat contracts entered into with the federal or state government, scenic restrictions entered into under the Scenic Easement Deed Act of 1959 (before January 1, 1975), open space easements granted under the Open-Space Easement Act of 1969 (before January 1, 1975), the Open-Space Easement Act of 1974 and the Regional Park and Open-Space District Laws: all are declared to be "enforceably restricted" according to the meaning of Article XIII, Section 8 and therefore eligible for the use-related assessment that Article XIII, Section 8 permits. For the purposes of the special assessment procedures set out in Sections 421–430.5, only property restricted by one of the methods just stated is considered enforceably restricted (§ 422).

In general, enforceably restricted open space lands, as defined, are to be valued by the capitalization of income method (§ 423). Sales data on comparable lands, even comparable enforceably restricted lands, may not be considered. Fair rental value, or, where sufficient rental information is lacking, an imputed amount "which the land being valued reasonably can be expected to yield under prudent management" consistent with the terms of its restrictions, will represent the gross revenue from the land (§ 423(a)). From this gross revenue, ordinary and necessary expenditures will be deducted. Revenue net of expenditures will be capitalized for tax purposes at a rate equal to the current yield rate for long-term U.S. government bonds factored by risk, property taxes and amortization of certain investments in perennials (§ 423(b)). The assessed value of the property will be the net income divided by the capitalization rate (§423(c)).

Unless a city or county objects to an adjustment, the valuation resulting from the income capitalization method will not be permitted to exceed the valuation that would result from the standard full-cash-value assessment method, which, due to Proposition 13 (Article XIIIA of the California Constitution), could under some circumstances prove to be lower than a use-related valuation (§ 423(d)).[162] In addition, to further offset the adverse effect of Proposition 13 on the attractiveness of entering into a voluntary land restriction, Section 423.3 was added to the Revenue and Taxation Code in 1980. It provides that local governments may elect, in lieu of income capitalization, to value properties restricted by Williamson Act or wildlife habitat contracts at anywhere from 70 to 90 percent of their unrestricted base year value, depending on the quality of the land involved (ranging from urban prime agricultural land to non-prime land).

Commercial timberland subject to an open space easement or Williamson Act contract is valued by imputing to it the present value of the income that the future harvests of timber can reasonably be expected to yield, subject to a $2-per-acre minimum (§ 423.5).

Section 426 provides a method for valuing lands for which a notice of nonrenewal has been served. When a notice of nonrenewal has been served or, if a landowner protests nonrenewal, when less than six years remain until an enforceable restriction will expire, restricted land will be valued each year according to a scale that takes into account the present discounted value attributable to the relative proximity of the time when the land will be free of restriction.

A prerequisite to valuation under Sections 421–430.5 is that enforceable restrictions must be signed, accepted and recorded on or before the lien date for the fiscal year to which the valuation would apply (§ 430.5).

RELATED PROPERTY TAX ASSESSMENT LEGISLATION

Timberlands within Timberland Production Zones (Rev. & Tax. Code §§ 431–437). Sections 431–437 provide for the valuation of timberlands within timberland production zones. Timberlands are valued according to periodically adjusted schedules relating to land quality and operability for timber harvesting (§ 434.5). Comparable sales data may be used in setting the schedules as long as the sales were of timberlands similarly restricted under a timberland production zone (§ 434.5(d)(2)). A $20-per-acre minimum value is presumed (§ 434.5(g)). Values attributable to compatible uses of the timberland, as well as values represented by minerals and other resources on the land, will be added to the discounted timber harvest values in arriving at the value of timberland (§ 435).

Lands Subject to Wildlife Habitat Contracts (Rev. & Tax. Code § 423.7). Lands subject to wildlife habitat contracts are to be valued according to an average current per-acre value based on recent sales of lands or undivided interests in lands subject to wildlife habitat contracts within the same county (§ 423.7).

Historical Property (Rev. & Tax. Code § 439–439.4). Historical property subject to an historical property contract pursuant to Government Code Section 50280 is valued according to the income capitalization method (§ 439.2).

ASSESSMENT VALUATION OF SECTION 815 CONSERVATION EASEMENTS

The designation in Section 422 of the Revenue and Taxation Code of those open space land restrictions to be considered enforceable restrictions qualifying for automatic use-related property tax assessment is exclusive; no other restrictions qualify, including conservation easements created solely under the Conservation Easements Act (Civ. Code § 815). The principal difference between a Section 815 conservation easement and a Section 51070 open space easement is the requirement of governmental participation in the latter. Presumably, the legislature intended that local governments have the opportunity to exercise some control over the effect of automatic use-related assessment on their tax bases.

An early draft of the Conservation Easements Act, however, did impose the express rebuttable presumption that conservation easements represented enforceable restrictions on land under Section 402.1 of the Revenue and Taxation Code.[163] The effect of that presumption would have been to require assessors to equate the value of restricted property to the value attributable to permitted uses of the property, unless it could be shown that the conservation easement had no effect on the market value of the property as compared to unrestricted lands. This provision did not appear in the final Act, at least in part because Proposition 13 had been approved in the meantime, reducing the immediate pressure for property tax relief.[164] However, the legislative history of the Conservation Easements Act indicates that the legislature intended any decline in market value resulting from the grant of a conservation easement to be reflected in subsequent assessments of the property restricted by the easement. As one committee analyst put it, "to the extent that an easement authorized by A.B. 245 caused a decline in property value, the owner would be entitled to a reduced assessment."[165]

Under Article XIII of the California Constitution, except as otherwise provided for, property is to be valued for tax purposes at its fair market value. Article XIIIA 2(b) of the California Constitution authorizes assessors to take "factors causing a decline in value" into account. In addition, Section 402.1, unlike Section 422, is not exclusive by its terms and mandates that the effect on land value of any enforceable restriction must be considered for assessment purposes. However, because there is no statute or regulation expressly governing the assessment valuation of lands subject to Section 815 conservation easements, and because few, if any, assessors have had experience with conservation easements, it is safe to predict that assessors will be most reluctant to consider the effect of conservation easements on land values. Particularly in light of the straitened financial circumstances besetting most local governments these days, persuading assessors to take account of the decline in market value caused by conservation easements is likely to require a painstaking marshaling of proofs and legal arguments as well as dogged persistence.

Whether there ought to be a reduction in assessed values will depend on many circumstances unique to the land involved. There will be cases, for example, where conservation easements enhance rather than reduce the market value of the property. However, development potential is typically such an important element of land value that its relinquishment from land otherwise suitable for development ought to lead to a lowered assessed value, unless the assessed value of the property as determined under Article XIIIA of the California Constitution is already so far below current market value that the reduction caused by the easement does not reach it. Appraisals used to determine the amount of a deduction for federal income tax purposes, although certainly not conclusive, may be useful evidence for justifying a reduction in property taxes.

IMPACT OF PROPOSITION 13

Proposition 13, proposed by initiative, was approved by the electorate on June 6, 1978, and became law as Article XIIIA of the California Constitution. Article XIIIA limits the amount of *ad valorem* tax that can be assessed on real property to 1 percent of the property's 1975–1976 assessed value or of its appraised value when subsequently purchased, newly constructed or subjected to a change in ownership. Adjustment for inflation cannot exceed 2 percent per year.

Proposition 13 represented an immediate tax relief measure of enormous dimension, leading to a property tax reduction of 50 to 60 percent for most properties.[166] As a result, the tax relief incentives built into the Williamson Act and the Open-Space Easement Act became, momentarily at least, much less compelling. Although prior to the passage of Proposition 13 open space tax relief had held down taxes on restricted land while assessments based on market value had greatly increased the tax burden on unrestricted land, after passage the difference between taxes realized on restricted and unrestricted property was vastly reduced and in some instances even eliminated.[167] Legislative steps have been taken to reinstate some of the pre-Proposition 13 tax advantage of the Williamson Act (Rev. & Tax. Code § 423.3), but no such action has been taken with regard to the Open-Space Easement Act.

Although the immediate effect of Article XIIIA was to close the gap between restricted and unrestricted properties, its long-range effect will not be uniform. Updated base year values will, over time, reestablish a relatively higher tax yield from unrestricted properties. In the meantime, fluctuations in the variables employed in calculating use-related values may determine the advantage, if any, of use-related valuation for open space lands. For example, changes in interest rates and crop prices will significantly affect the relative benefit to be derived from using the income capitalization method for assessing farmlands. In periods of high interest rates, use-related valuation should yield a substantially lower assessed value than would a market value approach. In periods of higher prices and relatively low interest rates, however, the advantage of a use-related valuation approach may be negligible or nonexistent.[168]

It is likely to be some time before the difference in treatment between restricted and unrestricted properties again becomes as significant as it was prior to Proposition 13. Future land conservation decisions with respect to unrestricted lands that do not change ownership over long periods of time, such as corporately owned properties, are likely to be made with little or no regard to their property tax effects. However, as time goes by, there is likely to be renewed incentive for landowners to restrict properties that have changed ownership and been exposed to current cash-value assessment valuation. The 1 percent tax rate limitation and the 2 percent inflation factor under Article XIIIA will protect unrestricted properties to some extent, but the high market value of land in California can only lead to increasingly higher taxes compared to use-related valuation. Although the burden of property taxes may now be a less important factor in a private land conservation decision than it has been historically, it is likely again to become an important factor for many individuals in the not too distant future.

Welfare Tax Exemption (Rev. & Tax. Code § 214); Special Provision for Open Space Lands (Rev. & Tax. Code § 214.02)

Article XIII, Section 4 of the California Constitution empowers the legislature to exempt from taxation property owned by nonprofit organizations and used exclusively for religious, hospital and charitable purposes. Section 214 of the Revenue and Taxation Code establishes the criteria for this "welfare exemption." Under the terms of Section 214, property owned by nonprofit organizations that is irrevocably dedicated to a charitable purpose is exempt from taxation.

In addition to the general welfare exemption provided by Section 214, Section 214.02 of the Revenue and Taxation Code provides, for the present, that property used for the preservation of native plants, animals or biotic communities, or geological formations of scientific or educational interest, or open space lands used for recreation and owned by qualified conservation organizations are exempt from taxation. To qualify, the property is required to be open to the general public, subject only to reasonable restrictions concerning the needs of the land. This special welfare exemption, as originally enacted in 1971, carried a sunset provision that would have rendered it inoperative after the lien date in 1981. In 1982, this expiration date was extended through the lien date in 1987, making the exemption operative, presumably, through the 1987–1988 fiscal year.[169] However, with the growing acceptance of open space protection as a charitable purpose, the general welfare exemption may be sufficient by itself to insulate from taxation those properties owned by nonprofit organizations and used for open space purposes.

The recent case of *Santa Catalina Island Conservancy v. County of Los Angeles*[170] is strong authority for this proposition. In upholding the Santa Catalina Island Conservancy's Section 214.02 exemption on its 40,000-acre island preserve, the court stated that in light of numerous legislatively promoted policies favoring open space protection, "It thus appears that nonprofit organizations formed and conducted for the purpose of preserving natural environments and recreational opportunities for the benefit of the public come within the term 'charitable' as defined by the decisions of our Supreme Court by lessening the burdens of government."[171] The court even indicated that the Conservancy's preservation of the unique Santa Catalina Island environment "in an era of scarce and vanishing ecological resources" constituted a sufficient charitable purpose irrespective of the fact that the Conservancy also happened to provide recreational opportunities on the island.

The welfare exemption should be available to shield from taxation whatever economic value a conservation easement may hold for a nonprofit grantee just as it would be for fee interests. However, it should not be necessary to invoke its protection. The general rule in California is that less-than-fee interests, including easements, are not assessed separately from the underlying fee unless the underlying fee is in public ownership.[172] The owner of land subject to a conservation easement or any other partial interest remains solely liable for all taxes related to the land regardless of any interests in his property, however valuable, others may hold. It is up to the parties involved to apportion this liability as they see fit, and, with respect to conservation easements, which generally are of little or no economic value to their holders, it is appropriate that the entire property tax burden should be borne by the landowner.

CHAPTER THREE

DRAFTING THE
CONSERVATION EASEMENT

The conservation easement is relatively simple conceptually, but assuring its effectiveness over time presents a drafting problem of considerable complexity for the parties involved and their attorneys. The purpose of a conservation easement is to protect specific conservation values on a given parcel of land, most often in perpetuity. If the condition of the land existing at the time of an easement grant could be frozen forever, this would present little difficulty, but land and land ownership are dynamic by nature. Change, both in the land itself and the uses appropriate to it, is inevitable. Unlike independent landowners, however, neither the grantor nor the grantee of a conservation easement has complete freedom to manage the restricted land to accommodate to change. Theirs is a shared control, approached from potentially competing perspectives. The challenge facing the drafter of a conservation easement is to make the instrument both sufficiently certain in its restrictions to assure protection of the conservation values involved and sufficiently flexible to meet the unforeseen changes in circumstances that are likely to occur over time.

Changes that are consistent with the purpose of a conservation easement can pose no threat to it. The real issue, though, is how and by whom the question of consistency is to be decided. There is no one wholly satisfactory solution to this problem. The nature of the parties and the land in question, the degree of protection desired and the type of easement involved: all will influence the choices made by the drafter. A "forever wild" natural ecosystem easement will be approached one way, an agricultural easement another. In the former case, for example, it may make sense to give a suitably qualified grantee sole discretion to determine what accommodations to change are consistent with the purpose of the easement; in the latter, it may not. Similarly, a landowner may be willing under some circumstances to give a nonprofit organization a higher degree of control than he would be willing to give a governmental entity. Because to do so would make the easement illusory, a grantor cannot retain for himself and his successors the sole right to determine the consistency question. He may, however, preserve a say in the matter by leaving it to future negotiation, arbitration or, if necessary, litigation. Whatever the approach taken, the competency and commitment of the grantee is likely to be the best check on the propriety of any given modification in light of an easement's underlying purpose. If a conservation easement is to endure, it is essential that both parties have a clear understanding of that purpose and that it be articulated in the easement document in a way that will be understood by future generations. The clearer the easement document itself is about the values to be protected, the less room there will be for dispute when changes occur.

Before drafting the easement, the conservation values of the land in question should be identified with care and specificity. Although doing so may involve substantial expenditures of time, effort and money, the parties should undertake to document and inventory these values. Maps, sketches, aerial photographs and reports describing the location of important features on the land should be compiled to establish the condition of the property at the time of the grant. Done properly, this property evaluation should serve as a reference point for designing the specific terms of the easement in a way that will accommodate the resource values of the land with the continuing and productive use of the land by its owner.

The conservation easement should be structured around the following basic terms:

□ a generalized statement of the purpose of the easement

□ reference to the specific conservation values of the land involved

□ a list of specific rights given the grantee to enable it to enforce the easement

□ a list of specific restrictions on undesirable activities to be reasonably anticipated

□ a general restriction on all other uses inconsistent with the intent and purpose of the easement

□ a list of specific uses or rights to be permitted or retained by the grantor

☐ a general reservation in the grantor of all other rights not inconsistent with the intent and purpose of the easement

Other features, such as requiring the grantee's consent as a precondition to engaging in certain particularly sensitive activities, should be considered as circumstances dictate.

In general, some care should be taken to see that the terms of the easement are not too tightly drawn. An easement that is too restrictive, that tries to be too comprehensive, may create too heavy a burden for the grantee in policing the easement and end up being more intrusive than need be upon the landowner's enjoyment of his land. On the other hand, an easement instrument that errs on the side of brevity and simplicity may fail in its purpose when adverse circumstances arise that should have been anticipated. A middle ground should be sought by employing both specific and general provisions in a complementary way.

Following is an annotated checklist of elements commonly found in conservation easements. Conservation easements range across a wide spectrum of purposes—from the protection of natural ecosystems to providing recreational open space to the perpetuation of farming on prime agricultural lands—and the content of a conservation easement will vary according to where on the spectrum the easement lies. In addition, the easement content will vary according to what statutory criteria, including federal and state tax laws, are relevant to it. Most important, the terms of a carefully drafted easement will need to conform to the characteristics of the land it is designed to protect. It is hoped that this checklist, in conjunction with the sample easement provided in Appendix 2, will serve as a useful starting place for those charged with the task of devising workable and lasting conservation easements to meet their particular needs.

CONSERVATION EASEMENT CHECKLIST

1 PARTIES

The easement should begin by identifying both the grantor and grantee. Identification of the grantor should show that he is the owner of the land in question and that he has the power to transfer the rights represented by the easement. If the land is community property, both husband and wife must join in the grant. In identifying the grantee, its state of incorporation, nonprofit status and qualification to do business in California should be shown. In addition, the grantee must be shown to be qualified to hold a conservation easement under the applicable California legislation—either the Open-Space Easement Act, the Conservation Easements Act or the Scenic Easement Deed Act—and the federal tax deduction section. As the requirements for these statutes vary, care must be taken to show that the grantee fits the exact statutory requirements applicable to the easement in question. The addresses of the grantor and grantee should be shown also.

2 LEGAL AND QUALITATIVE DESCRIPTION OF THE PROPERTY

The legal description of the property can be given at this point or as part of the grant section. Some descriptive phrase identifying the property should be given parenthetically to the legal description and used throughout the easement document to identify the property. A popular name associated with the land (e.g., "Tara") or simply "the Protected Property" might be used. Following the legal description of the property, the "story" of the land should be told, identifying the conservation values to be protected by the easement. A description of the recreational, scenic, ecological or other open space values of the land should be drafted in a way that underscores the land's importance as a local, regional or national open space resource. This description provides a rationale for the protective measures to follow.

3 TYPE AND PURPOSE OF EASEMENT

The type of easement involved (e.g., open space, conservation or scenic) and the purpose of the easement (e.g., to protect a relatively natural ecosystem or to preserve agricultural open space pursuant to a local watershed management program) must be set forth. Specific details relating to the property in question should be given if appropriate. Again, care must be taken to meet all applicable statutory criteria, especially the qualified purpose requirement of the federal tax deduction section. The language of the relevant statutes should be tracked rather closely, and, with regard to the federal tax deduction, particular care should be taken to illustrate the public benefit to be derived from the easement. Express reference should be made to the governing statute or statutes, and their purposes and authority, along with a recital that the easement meets all statutory requirements and is created pursuant to the applicable statutes.

4 STATEMENT OF INTENT OF GRANTOR AND GRANTEE

The intent of the grantor in giving the easement should be clearly stated and should be shown to begin with a general charitable motive for preservation of open space that has led to a specific desire to protect the subject property and the conservation values that have been identified on the property. The expression of general charitable intent will enable a court, if necessary, to perpetuate the overall conservation purpose of the easement even if changed circumstances should make certain specific requirements or purposes of the easement impossible to carry out. The intention of the grantor to create an easement running with the land for the protection of specified conservation values should be clearly set forth. The grantee's intention to honor, in perpetuity or for the term stated, the intentions of the grantor and to carry out the protection and preservation of the land according to the purpose and terms of the easement should be stated as well.

The statement of purpose and intent is the touchstone of the easement. Any change in kind or degree of the use to be made of the land must be tested for consistency with the purpose and intent of the easement before it can be permitted. The statement of purpose and intent should be drafted with this central functional role in mind.

5 REFERENCE TO DOCUMENTATION OF CONSERVATION VALUES TO BE PRESERVED

To the extent possible, resource inventories, maps, reports, aerial photographs and other scientific documentation should be incorporated in the easement as concrete evidence of the conservation values that the grantor and grantee intend to preserve. Such documentation provides an objective base line for determining the consistency of any future actions on the land with the purposes of the easement, as well as for evaluating the efficacy of the grantee's enforcement of the easement over time. Because nature is dynamic, and the interrelationships affecting change within an ecosystem are complex and subtle—originating both within and without the ecosystem itself—it would, of course, be foolish to attempt to freeze the natural development of the land in order to perpetuate whatever stage the land happens to be in at the time the easement is granted. This would be an artificial and self-defeating approach to conservation. Nevertheless, adequate documentation regarding the state of the land at the time the easement is granted provides a common reference point from which adaptation to future natural or human changes on the land can proceed.

The grantee's commitment to continuously monitor the interrelationship between natural and human systems on the land can be stated here. In addition, a requirement for periodic renewal of the documentation file should be included. The use of general terms throughout the easement to describe conservation values on the land could be defined here as meaning those values identified in the documentation.

6 GRANT OF EASEMENT

This section is the operative section of the easement document. It contains the words of conveyance that effect the transfer of the easement interest, recites whatever consideration supports the grant (including the terms of the easement itself) and sets forth the duration of the easement (perpetuity or term of years). If a term easement under the Open-Space Easement Act is given, the grant also must provide for automatic annual renewal. Both the Conservation Easements Act and the federal tax deduction section require that an easement be perpetual.

7 RIGHTS, RESTRICTIONS, PERMITTED USES AND RESERVATIONS

The heart of the easement instrument is that part following the grant that sets forth the rights, restrictions, permitted uses and reservations that will govern the future of the land. These sections determine the force and substance of the easement. They must be clearly thought through and clearly drafted if the easement is to be well understood by the parties and enforceable as they intend. The parties should have the clearest possible picture of what is forbidden and what is allowed.

As with all easement terms, these sections will be the subject of negotiation between the grantor and the grantee at the time the easement is granted, and, depending on the type and purpose of the easement, they may be broadly permissive or quite restrictive. How the rights and restrictions are drafted, however, greatly influences the question of deductibility of the easement as well as its monetary value and its long-range efficacy.

Rights of the Grantee. The grantee must be given all powers necessary to monitor and enforce compliance with the terms of the easement and to fulfill the grantee's role as guardian of the conservation values involved. Consideration should be given to the following:

☐ In general, the grantee is given the right to identify, preserve and protect the conservation values of the property and to have the property maintained in its natural, scenic or open space condition.

☐ The grantee must be given the right to enter the property in a reasonable manner for the purpose of inspection to assure that the grantor or his successors are complying with the terms of the easement. The grantee also may be given the right of entry for other purposes, such as scientific study, if such entry is desired by the parties. Notice prior to entry may be required.

☐ The grantee must be given the right to enforce the easement by the concurrent remedies of injunction (both mandatory and prohibitive) and damages, as authorized by the applicable California statute. A notice period may, but need not, be required before bringing an enforcement action. The grantee also should be given the power to require the restoration of the protected property at the grantor's expense in the event that it is damaged by the grantor. The grantee should be given the discretion to determine how and when to enforce the easement, but such discretion should be made subject to and controlled by the clear intent and purpose of the easement. Any third party enforcement right, as is, for example, provided by Section 51086 of the Open-Space Easement Act, should be expressly stated. The easement should state that any failure by the grantee to exercise its rights should not be construed as a waiver of those rights.

☐ Depending on the intentions of the parties and the resources and commitment of the grantee, additional affirmative rights may be given to the grantee to enhance the conservation values of the property or to actively maintain those values. In most easements, however, the grantee will be without the resources to play any more active role than that of inspector and enforcer.

☐ If public access to the easement area is to be granted, it should be so stated in this section. If public entry is to be prohibited or confined to specific purposes or times, the limitations on entry should be clearly stated.

Restrictions. Restrictions on all activities foreseeably harmful to the conservation values of the easement should be set forth with specificity. The restrictions to be placed on use of the land will vary depending on the type of easement involved and the nature of the land in question. A "forever wild" natural ecosystem easement should prohibit all uses except those of the very lowest intensity, such as, where appropriate, hiking and riding. A scenic easement would likely permit more uses than a natural ecosystem easement, insuring only that permitted uses preserve the view. Agricultural, forest and grazing open space easements should have restrictions tailored specifically to those uses. Of course, a particular easement may combine features of more than one type. The possibilities are endless, and the particular circumstances of the property in question will determine the actual restrictions imposed. Following are suggested restrictions for three basic types of conservation easements.

Natural Ecosystem Easements. Natural ecosystem easements are likely to be quite detailed, with restrictions carefully tailored to the sensitive ecological values designated for protection. Restrictions commonly encountered in such easements include:
☐ Prohibit all subdivision, construction or placement of buildings, utility lines and poles, camping accommodations, mobile homes or other portable living headquarters, signs and billboards. Provide for removal of existing structures immediately or within specified time, if desired.
☐ If wetlands are involved, prohibit all filling, dredging or diking.
☐ Prohibit mineral exploration, mining, drilling, logging, farming, excavation, removal of soil or other materials, building of roads or any other alteration in the topography except as necessary to establish or maintain authorized foot trails. Provide for reclamation, if desired.
☐ Prohibit dumping of trash, ashes, garbage or other unsightly

or offensive materials. If desired, provide for removal of existing dumps.

☐ Prohibit alteration or manipulation of water courses, lakes, ponds or other water bodies and prohibit any use that is detrimental to water quality.

☐ Prohibit the removal, destruction or cutting of trees, grasses or other vegetation except as necessary to control disease or fire or as a measure for rehabilitating a natural area. Alternatively, prohibit logging except pursuant to a mutually agreed upon plan based on sustained yield practices compatible with habitat protection.

☐ Prohibit the introduction of nonnative plant and animal species that may compete with and result in the decline or elimination of native species. Confine any new plantings to native plants characteristic of the region.

☐ Prohibit all chemical spraying of the area except as authorized by the grantee in accordance with the highest standards for protecting the ecosystem.

☐ Prohibit the use of motorized vehicles on land or water.

☐ Prohibit any use that would cause, increase or substantially add to the risk of erosion.

☐ Prohibit hunting or trapping except as authorized by the grantee for the purpose of maintaining animal populations in ecological balance.

☐ Prohibit the disturbance of any particularly sensitive areas (e.g., black hawk nesting site), as identified on maps incorporated by reference in the easement document.

☐ In general, prohibit all other uses unrelated to enjoyment of the natural values of the area (e.g., all uses except hiking, low-impact camping or limited riding).

Scenic Easements. A scenic easement might contain some of the same restrictions imposed by a natural ecosystem easement, such as prohibition of signs and billboards, prohibition of filling or diking wetlands, prohibitions against altering or manipulating natural water courses or water bodies, prohibitions against dumping, erosion-causing activities, mineral exploration or extraction, and the like. However, rather than prohibiting all development, the typical scenic easement would be more likely only to regulate the type and amount of subdivision and development that would be permitted in order to assure consistency with preservation of the scenic qualities of the land. Limitations on density, height, bulk and design of structures might be expressly stated. Active maintenance to preserve the view also should be provided for, including the cutting or pruning of obstructive vegetation and similar corrective measures.

Open Space Easements Involving Agricultural, Grazing and Forest Uses. Easements over property that will remain in productive uses should be drafted to restrict those activities that are unnecessary for the uses to be permitted and that would adversely affect the conservation values involved. All uses other than permitted uses should be prohibited, as necessary, and permitted uses should be held to the highest standards of the industry in question for husbanding the renewable land resources involved. Any change or extension of permitted uses might be made subject to prior approval by, and continuing consultation with, the grantee to assure protection of the conservation values of the easement. All aspects of any new project related to a permitted use might be made subject to review by the grantee to determine their effect on the easement values.

In addition to whatever specific restrictions are appropriate to a given easement, the easement document should contain a general prohibition of all activities that are inconsistent with the conservation values intended for protection. Depending on the intentions of the parties and the type of easement involved, an express power to determine what is consistent with the conservation values of the easement might be given to the grantee or might not be allocated at all, leaving the determination of consistency to negotiation, arbitration or, ultimately, the courts.

Because circumstances might arise in the future to justify engaging in some prohibited use on the property, provision might be made for allowing certain prohibited uses if undertaken after obtaining the prior express written consent of the grantee. Such consent should hinge on whether the use can be undertaken without significantly diminishing any of the conservation values intended for protection under the easement.

Permitted Uses and Reservations. Uses that are consistent with the intent and purpose of the easement should be expressly permitted by the terms of the easement along with those uses that might reasonably be anticipated as necessarily adjunct to the grantor's main permitted uses of the land. Depending on the nature of the easement, such uses might include: the building of a specified number of homes or other structures compatible with the values protected by the easement; development of water resources on the land; the right to lay pipes or conduits underground; the right to specified recreational use of certain water or other areas on the land; the right to make improvements to prevent flooding or disease; the right to remove diseased or dangerous trees or nonnative species of vegetation; the right to erect and maintain fences; the right to maintain existing houses and structures, to add to them as desired and to replace them if destroyed or damaged; the right to take measures necessary to prevent trespass (including posting the property); the right to continue existing uses on the land, such as ranching, farming or forestry, and to extend such uses as appropriate. Where specific activities not yet begun are anticipated, these activities should be clearly delineated. All other uses not inconsistent with the purpose of the easement should be reserved to the grantor.

Certain permitted uses, although reserved to the grantor as a matter of right, may be made subject to the grantee's approval of the manner in which they are carried out, including the nature, siting, size, capacity and number of any improvements involved. The easement instrument might state that the grantee may not unreasonably withhold any approval and might set forth a deadline by which decisions on requests to engage in such activities must be made.

8 ALLOCATION OF COSTS

The costs of maintenance, insurance, taxes, assessments and any liabilities related to the land subject to the easement should be borne by the grantor. Only if the grantee is intended to have a truly active role in maintaining the property under easement should it be required to share the costs of maintenance and insurance. Otherwise, the grantor should indemnify the grantee against incurring such costs.

The costs of regular inspection of the easement property, of monitoring compliance with the easement and of keeping all resource data current should be borne by the grantee. It should be noted that these costs can be significant. Fiscal constraints on governmental entities may put all but the simplest easements out of reach of many of them. As for nonprofit organizations, few of whom have extensive financial resources to call upon, it is not uncommon for them to request that landowners who are capable of it establish an endowment for offsetting the costs of monitoring easement compliance.

9 SUBSEQUENT DEEDS

A grantor should agree to incorporate the easement in any subsequent deed or other legal instrument by which he divests himself of the fee title or any possessory interest in the land. If duly recorded, the easement will be enforceable regardless of whether it is inserted in subsequent deeds because it will appear in the chain of title, thereby giving constructive notice to any future owner of the land. However, this requirement of insertion in a later deed does increase the likelihood that actual notice will be imparted to subsequent takers.

10 EXECUTORY LIMITATION

An executory limitation is a provision for forfeiture of the easement by the grantee to another qualified holder in the event the grantee should abandon or neglect to enforce the easement. Even without such a limitation, a court could, at the behest of the attorney general acting under his general supervisory powers over charitable institutions, assure that the purposes of the easement are carried out. However, the executory limitation creates an additional incentive to strictly enforce the easement. Acceptance of the future interest created by an executory limitation should be obtained from the organization named as successor to the grantee.

11 ASSIGNMENT

The easement instrument should state that the grantee will hold the easement exclusively for conservation purposes, as required by the federal deduction legislation, and that it will not transfer the easement except to an organization qualified to hold such interests under the relevant California and federal laws.

12 INTEGRATION

The easement instrument should provide that it is the final and complete expression of the agreement between the parties and that any and all oral agreements are merged into the written instrument. This provision may prevent avoidance of the terms of the easement by the assertion of some oral understanding not contained in the instrument.

13 SEVERABILITY

The instrument should state that if any of its provisions are declared invalid in the future, the remaining provisions will nonetheless remain in full force.

14 COSTS OF ENFORCEMENT

The grantor or his successor in interest should be required to pay all costs related to enforcing the easement, including the costs of attorney fees and any restoration of the property made necessary by the acts of the grantor.

15 HABENDUM CLAUSE

The instrument should recite that the grant has been made to the grantee "to have and to hold" to its use and that of its successors and assigns forever (or for the stated term) and that the terms, conditions, restrictions and purposes of the easement shall bind not only the grantor but his agents, personal representatives, heirs, assigns and all other successors in interest to him and shall continue as a servitude running with the land in perpetuity (or for the stated term).

16 DATE, SIGNATURES AND ACKNOWLEDGMENT

The parties to the easement must sign it, date it and have it acknowledged in accordance with California law. If the easement is granted to a nonprofit organization under the Open-Space Easement Act, a space should be provided for witnessing the approval of the easement by the relevant local governmental body. In addition, if desired, space might be provided for indicating the acceptance of an executory interest by a proposed successor grantee.

17 EXHIBITS

Any supporting maps, plans, surveys, photographs, reports or scientific documentation that are material to the easement should be attached as numbered exhibits and incorporated in the main body of the easement by reference to such numbers.

CHAPTER FOUR

CATALOG OF OTHER REAL PROPERTY CONSERVATION TECHNIQUES

Familiarity with the broad range of private real property interests and techniques available for use in land conservation serves to encourage a flexible and creative approach to the varied opportunities that arise in this field. Although this book focuses on conservation easements, a basic knowledge of other available techniques is essential to understanding where the conservation easement fits into the overall land conservation effort. This chapter catalogs a number of real property interests and techniques that can be used to further land conservation goals. The list is not exhaustive. The bibliography contains some useful sources of other techniques, and The Trust for Public Land, as well as the State Coastal Conservancy and The Nature Conservancy, can provide still more.

DEFEASIBLE FEE TECHNIQUES

For those conservation-minded landowners who are in a position to make a transfer of ownership, the simplest and most direct means of achieving land conservation goals is an outright grant of the full, unrestricted ownership of property (fee simple absolute) to an organization dedicated to land conservation. When a landowner's desire to perpetuate the conservation values of his own property is subordinate to his belief in the wider goals of land conservation, making an outright grant may be the best means of pursuing those goals. An outright grant enables a grantee organization to exercise its own judgment concerning how best to manage a parcel of land to serve its conservation purposes. As the unrestricted owner of the land, the conservation organization can respond to future changes and opportunities in the way it determines is best suited to its long-term goals. As long as a landowner has faith in his grantee's abilities and judgment, an outright grant should well serve his purposes.

Where, however, a landowner's desire for perpetual preservation of his own land is the central motivating factor in his decision to transfer it to a conservation organization or a governmental entity, and he does not wish to subordinate that desire to a broader conservation purpose, he may condition his grant upon the continuous maintenance of the land for specified conservation purposes. He can do so by granting not a fee simple absolute but a defeasible fee, a type of ownership that can be forfeited by the grantee's failure to perform specified conditions or by the occurrence of some specified event.

Ownership of a defeasible fee brings with it all the rights and privileges usually associated with outright ownership. The grantee of a defeasible fee and his successors can deal with the property in question as they please in perpetuity, so long as they honor the conditions placed upon the grant, or the event limiting the duration of the grant does not occur. If the conditions are breached or the specified event occurs, however, the property may, depending on the circumstances at the time, become revested in the grantor or his successor.

In the conservation context, a defeasible fee grant can operate much like a conservation easement to restrict land in perpetuity to conservation uses. In fact, the Conservation Easements Act defines a conservation easement broadly enough to include future interests created by defeasible fees.[173] Because of the potential severity of the penalty in the event of failure to observe the conditions attached to it—loss of the property—a defeasible fee may, in fact, be an even more potent tool than the typical conservation easement. For the same reason, however, use of defeasible fees is disfavored by the courts, and great care must be taken in their creation to assure their enforceability.

Because there is more than a little confusion surrounding the law of defeasible fees, a brief review of the terminology may prove helpful. Under the common law, there are three types of defeasible fees, two of them, known as the *fee subject to a condition subsequent* and the *fee simple determinable*, reserving a reversionary interest in the grantor, and a third, the *fee subject to an executory limitation*, creating a future interest in a third party. Like so much in the law governing real property, these interests are of ancient origin, and their validity turns on as refined a set of technicalities as the common law has ever devised. To achieve the result intended, very specific wording must be used. If the right words are not used, it is unlikely that a court will enforce the future interest involved.

A fee subject to a condition subsequent is created by use of obvious conditional language, such as "but if," "provided that" or "upon the express condition subsequent that," followed by the desired restriction. The future interest retained by the grantor of a condition subsequent deed is called a *right of reentry* or a *power of termination* and is freely transferable.[174] So that there is no doubt what the parties intend to be the consequence of a breach of a stated condition, it is advisable to expressly reserve this right or power in the language of the grant.[175] A fee subject to a condition subsequent grant might read: "To City, its successors and assigns, upon the express condition subsequent that if City or its successor in interest ever use the land or permit it to be used other than exclusively and perpetually as a wildlife preserve, the grantor may reenter and terminate the estate granted."

The same condition, however, could be expressed in durational language ("so long as," "until," "while," "during"). If the grantor should choose to do so, the estate created would be transformed from a fee subject to a condition subsequent into a fee simple determinable, and the future interest retained, still transferable, would become a *possibility of reverter*. Because this limitation is durational, no reference to the possibility of reverter need be made in the language of the grant. When the time established for the duration of an estate ends, reversion to the grantor is implied unless another intention has been expressed. The grant might read: "To City, its successors and assigns so long as the land is used exclusively as a wildlife preserve." As will be seen, although the identical underlying desire on the part of the landowner for the perpetual conservation use of his land is expressed by both clauses, the choice between conditional or durational language was, theoretically at least, an operative one under California law until most recently.

The one distinction under California law between the fee subject to a condition subsequent and the fee simple determinable—a distinction that had long since been severed from its medieval rationale—was in the consequences that were said to flow from the breach of the conditions imposed by each of them. Both were subject to termination upon the occurrence of a specified event or the breach of a specified condition, but the termination of a fee simple determinable was considered "automatic," whereas a fee subject to a condition subsequent terminated only if the grantor or his successor acted to enforce his reversionary rights. Undue delay in enforcing a power of termination might be construed by a court as a waiver, thereby voiding the interest.[176] Since technically a reverter was automatic, delay in enforcing it could not constitute a waiver. Nevertheless, although the threat of automatic forfeiture might have had a somewhat stronger restraining influence on a defeasible fee owner than the mere possibility of enforcing a power of termination, the distinction between the fee simple determinable and the fee subject to a condition subsequent, whatever its historical importance, was more theoretical than real.

In the event of breach, unless the owner of the terminated fee acquiesced in its forfeiture, a judicial action to quiet title would have been necessary to enforce the reversionary interest of the grantor or his successor in either case.[177] The five-year statute of limitations generally applicable to actions involving real property was apparently applicable to the enforcement of powers of termination.[178] It was not clear whether the statute was applicable to reverters, but the five-year period for adverse possession in California should have made the question largely academic. The person in possession ought to have had good title in five years in either case.[179] The result was that the automatic forfeiture feature of the fee simple determinable severely clouded title, regarding which clarity is an important public policy,[180] without adding anything of substance to the law of future interests.

In 1981, the California Law Revision Commission concluded a study of record interests affecting the marketability of title to real property and, finding "no practical difference of any substance" between the functionally identical possibility of reverter and power of termination, recommended that the fee simple determinable and the possibility of reverter be abolished in California as "unnecessary," particularly in light of the record problems they created.[181] In 1982, the California legislature followed this recommendation, collapsing the common law fee simple determinable and possibility of reverter, by statute, into the fee subject to a condition subsequent and power of termination, respectively.[182] Henceforth, whether a grant is expressed in durational or conditional language, the contingent future interest of the grantor of a defeasible fee will be treated as a power of termination following a fee subject to a condition subsequent. In addition, the legislature, again on the recommendation of the Law Revision Commission, imposed a thirty-year limit on the duration of powers of termination and the land use restrictions they impose. A power of termination can, however, be renewed indefinitely for successive thirty-year periods by recording a notice of intent to preserve the interest prior to expiration.[183] To eliminate any uncertainty, the legislature also provided that an absolute five-year statute of limitations governs actions to enforce powers of termination in the event of breach.[184]

The thirty-year renewal requirement for powers of termination assures that only a power in which someone preserves an active interest will remain a burden on title.[185] The requirement creates a critical administrative task for holders of powers of termination to insure that their interests are kept current. However, there are, for our purposes, two important classes of holders who are exempt from this requirement: state and local public entities and holders of conservation easements that take the form of powers of termination.[186] This last is an important recognition of the overriding public benefit of long-term land controls when used for conservation purposes.

As previously stated, there is a third type of defeasible fee, the fee subject to an executory limitation. This interest is created by the use of either conditional or durational language with an express designation of a third person, instead of the grantor, to take the property in the event of a breach. The future interest created by an executory limitation is called simply an *executory interest.* As with the now obsolete fee simple determinable, forfeiture is automatic upon the occurrence of a triggering event or breach of a specified condition. An executory limitation might read : "To City, its successors and assigns, but if the land shall ever be used other than as a wildlife preserve, then to The Trust for Public Land."

Unlike the power of termination, which California law treats as a "vested" reversionary interest retained by the grantor, an executory interest is not considered a vested interest. It is beyond the scope of this book to explore the esoteric law of vesting, but the consequence of the distinction is that an executory limitation is subject to a common law rule called "the rule against perpetuities," which voids contingent future interests if there is a possibility that they may not vest (roughly, become certain) until the too remote or indefinite future—in California, twenty-one years after the death of a relevant person or, alternatively, sixty years.[187] However, an executory limitation to a charitable organization following the grant of a defeasible interest to another charitable organization is recognized as an exception to the rule against perpetuities and will be upheld.[188] Executory interests, classified simply as remainders in California, are freely transferable.[189]

In the use of defeasible fees, the greatest obstacle to be overcome, as intimated earlier, is the abhorrence of the courts for the severe forfeiture penalty. There is a preference in our law for the free use of property, certainty of title and freedom from burdensome controls on property imposed by past generations. For a court to recognize a defeasible fee it must be convinced that it has no alternative. The grant of a defeasible fee must be so clearly drafted, so free of ambiguity, as to leave no room for any contrary judicial construction.

A forfeiture clause is strictly construed against the party to be benefited by it.[190] As the California Supreme Court has stated: "No provision in a deed relied on to create a condition subsequent will be so interpreted if the language of the provision will bear any other reasonable construction."[191] Given the slightest opening, the courts will strain to find that a condition is a mere declaration of purpose or a personal covenant or trust not binding between successors to the original parties, or, if binding as a restrictive covenant, not enforceable by forfeiture. Even where a court is forced to recognize a defeasible fee, it will construe the restriction narrowly to avoid finding that there has been a breach. Finally, a court may find, even where a defeasible fee has been breached, that the condition has been waived or other considerations militate against its enforcement, including a change in surrounding circumstances.[192] The intent to create a defeasible fee binding on successors for all time must be expressed unequivocally if the interest intended is to succeed in running this gauntlet of strict construction. Only a properly drafted defeasible fee, showing the "clear and unmistakable intention" of the parties to create it, will be enforced.[193]

Defeasible fees may prove useful conservation tools under some circumstances. If limited to those situations in which an especially powerful deterrent is felt to be necessary to protect conservation values, the inhibiting effect of the threat of forfeiture inherent in a defeasible fee may be worth the lack of flexibility of the device. If the future interest is granted to some "watchdog agency,"[194] public or private, that shares the conservation goals of the grantor, the conservation purpose of a grant is further strengthened and greater assurance that it will be honored in perpetuity is derived.

A transaction incorporating a future interest in favor of a conservation organization may be structured in several different ways. An executory limitation may be used as long as the executory interest in the conservation organization follows a defeasible fee to another charitable organization or to a governmental entity. If it does not, the rule against perpetuities will void the limitation. If the grantee of the fee is not a charitable or governmental entity, the grantor can avoid the rule against perpetuities by reserving a power of termination in himself and then transferring that reversionary interest to a conservation organization. Alternatively, he could transfer a fee simple absolute to the conservation organization under an agreement that the conservation organization would, in turn, transfer it to some predetermined third party after reserving a reversionary interest in itself. The transaction could be structured with sufficient detail to comply with the terms of the Conservation Easements or Open-Space Easement Acts, resulting in the creation of an interest that would function much like a typical conservation easement but, because of the forfeiture provision, with an even stronger bite.

Even though the possibility exists that the property given may return to the grantor, a defeasible fee gift is deductible under the federal tax laws.[195] The income tax regulations state that where a gift of property presently vested can be defeated only by a subsequent act or event "so remote as to be negligible," a deduction will be allowed.[196] The example is given in the regulations of a conditional gift of land to a city for park purposes where the city does, in fact, intend to use the land for a park. Likewise, the fact that a grant of a defeasible fee is technically a gift of a partial interest in property will not defeat it; for tax purposes it is treated as a gift of the donor's entire interest.[197] A condition restricting the use of land may, however, affect the value of the gift and therefore the amount of the allowable deduction.[198] To preserve the full value of a defeasible fee gift and thereby maximize his deduction, a donor should consider either transferring his reversionary interest or making an executory limitation to a tax-exempt organization.

FULL FEE TECHNIQUES

Landowners who are willing to part with title to their lands unconditionally in favor of governmental entities or conservation organizations may, nevertheless, be unable for any number of reasons to make an outright donation of the full fee simple absolute title to their property or to find a conservation-minded buyer capable of paying full market value for property to be dedicated to a conservation use. There are a number of techniques available to allow a landowner to remain in possession of his property, if that is his concern, or to structure a sale or mixed sale/donation so as to make the transaction economically feasible for both the landowner and the conservation organization or governmental buyer/donee. These techniques can help the seller to spread or reduce capital gains taxes or maximize deductions while lightening the buyer's burden of funding major acquisitions. The following is a sampling of available techniques. They may be used separately or in combination as desired.

Purchase and Lease-back or Sell-back Arrangement

In a purchase and lease-back arrangement a landowner sells his land but continues to use it as the buyer's tenant. The purchase and lease-back enables the landowner to realize the capital gain from the sale of his appreciated property and at the same time remain in possession of the land. The buyer organization acquires land that it considers important for its present conservation values or for some planned future recreational or open space use at a time when it is able to fund such a purchase. The buyer gains full control over the destiny of the land and at the same time assures itself of a steady stream of rental income. The buyer may impose any restrictions it considers appropriate for protection of the land in the lease granted to the seller, and the lease may be as detailed in its restrictions as a conservation easement would be. In addition, the lease agreement should be used to allocate all the rights and duties of the parties, including the payment of property taxes and maintenance costs. Although the seller/lessee normally bears the burden of maintenance costs, such costs may be shared if appropriate.

A landowner can, if he is so disposed, either donate the property outright and lease it back or make a partial donation by way of a bargain sale.[199] As long as the rental payments are set at fair market value, the landowner will receive a charitable deduction for the contribution. If rents are not set at fair market value, the deduction for the donation might be reduced or disallowed on the ground that the landowner has not parted with his entire interest in the property.[200]

A seller might find a purchase and lease-back arrangement attractive because of the cash it would free up and, if the seller is a business, because the expense of rental payments might provide it with a needed deduction. In addition, the arrangement might be especially useful to governmental entities engaged in long-term land use planning by enabling them to acquire strategic properties at current prices and reserve them for future use without incurring maintenance costs. At the same time, the property purchased would become a productive source of regular income to the government. The purchase and lease-back technique was recognized as appropriate for governmental entities in 1959 in the Scenic Easement Deed Act, which expressly empowers counties and cities to use this method for preserving open space lands.[201]

As an alternative to leasing back the property, the buyer could sell it back subject to desired restrictions. The interest retained would closely resemble a typical conservation easement, except that, if the sale back is of a defeasible fee, the restrictions involved might be made subject to a forfeiture provision. Purchase and sell-backs are used by the State Coastal Conservancy to protect agricultural lands within the coastal zone.[202]

Bargain Sale

A landowner who is financially incapable of making an outright gift of his property to a conservation organization or governmental entity may nevertheless find it to his advantage to make a partial gift of his property for conservation purposes. Use of the bargain sale technique improves his chances of finding a conservation-oriented buyer who will be able to afford his price. In a bargain sale, the landowner receives an immediate substantial cash payment for his property and at the same time, for the bargain element, receives a charitable deduction and avoids capital gains taxes.

To be assured of bargain sale treatment by the IRS, a competent written appraisal must be made of the property in order to determine the amount of the bargain element. The landowner must express his intent to make a donation of the difference between the fair market value of the property and the sale price in the contract of sale in order to preserve his eligibility for a deduction. The difference between fair market value and the sale price will determine the value of the gift, which, depending on the amount of the gift and the status of the donee, may be fully deductible. Capital gains taxes on the gift portion are avoided. The landowner must, however, pay a capital gains tax on the gain received from the sale portion of the transaction.[203]

In order to determine what portion of the amount received is taxable, the landowner must allocate his basis in the property between the gift and sale portions proportionately. The percentage of the basis to be allocated to the sale price is equal to the percentage of the fair market value of the property that the sale price represents. For example, a landowner who sells property with a fair market value of $100,000 to a nonprofit organization at his cost in the property of $60,000 (60 percent of fair market value) will receive a charitable deduction of $40,000 and pay a capital gains tax on the amount received in excess of 60 percent of the sale price: 60 percent of $60,000 = $36,000; $60,000 − $36,000 = $24,000. His taxable gain is $24,000.[204]

The bargain element can be infused into any transaction where consideration is received for property granted to a nonprofit organization. Even in a tax-free transaction, such as an exchange of "like kind" business or investment property under Internal Revenue Code Section 1031(a), a bargain element could play an important role. Commercial real estate could be exchanged for open space lands giving a landowner income-producing property in exchange for unproductive land with open space values. Attracted by this income element and the availability of a charitable deduction for any difference between the fair market values of the properties exchanged, a landowner might be willing to accept income-producing property that has a lower fair market value than the open space property given up.[205]

The bargain sale technique is an economically attractive method for landowners to make property with significant conservation values available to conservation organizations at greatly reduced prices.

Installment Sale

The installment sale method provides a conservation-minded buyer with a means of spreading the cost of purchasing important land areas. The conservation-minded buyer can control the use of the land in question at a fraction of the cost of an up-front purchase and at the same time insulate itself against inflation and subsequent appreciation by freezing the price at the time of entering into an installment sale agreement. The seller benefits from spreading his capital gains tax over the term of the agreement, thereby minimizing the effect of the progressive tax structure by reducing the gain attributable to any one year.

The installment sale may be structured to provide that the buyer agree to purchase the entire property and pay for it in periodic installments spread over a substantial period of time, either taking title at once subject to a mortgage interest in the seller or receiving legal title to the property at such time as the final installment payment is made. Alternatively, the buyer could agree to purchase a portion of the land each year and take title to that portion as payment is made for it. Purchase of the remaining portions could be obligatory or optional as desired. In either case, the agreement negotiated by the parties could provide that the landowner remain in possession of the property prior to the transfer of title, subject to restrictions on use for the preservation of conservation values. Where the landowner remains in possession, maintenance costs and property taxes may be allocated to him.

At one time the installment sale technique was used to spread charitable deductions over a period of years through the cancellation of installment indebtedness as each installment fell due. Recent changes in the Internal Revenue Code have made this procedure unattractive to taxpayers. Note cancellations are now treated as taxable events, and the capital gain element of the installment due is taxed in the year that the installment debt is forgiven.[206] An installment sale could be structured, however, to contain a bargain sale element, in which case some spreading of the deduction over time might be possible. Where a definite portion of the land under contract is purchased with each installment, the bargain element of each installment payment would be deductible in the year that the payment is made.[207] This feature of an installment bargain sale can be conjoined with the five-year carry-over available for most kinds of charitable gifts[208] to maximize the deduction available for large gifts of land.

Sale or Gift of an Undivided Interest in Land

The sale or donation of an undivided interest in land to a conservation organization is another technique by which a landowner may remain in possession of his property while effectively restricting its use. When a person obtains an undivided interest in land he becomes an owner of a fractional share of the entire property. Each owner of an undivided interest is free to transfer his share as he sees fit. Owners of undivided interests are called tenants-in-common, and each is entitled to possession and enjoyment of the whole property in proportion to his interest in the property. Frequently, these rights are allocated on a seasonal basis.[209] A cotenant conservation organization need not use its possession entitlement, but, unless otherwise agreed, it will be responsible for a percentage of all expenses related to the property equal to its percentage of ownership. Both the landowner and conservation organization have a say in how the property is to be used. Should they not be able to agree, each of them as cotenants has the right to sue to physically divide the property or force its sale to effect a "partition" of their interests. This possibility could make the undivided interest approach a precarious conservation technique under some circumstances. However, if the parties take care to set out the terms of their relationship in a detailed cotenancy agreement, the risk of the arrangement ending unhappily will be greatly reduced.

The phased sale of land through the periodic grant of undivided interests to a conservation organization is a useful technique for spreading both the gain and cost involved in the sale of land over a long period. The approach is, however, most useful as a means of spreading a charitable deduction over time to maximize its benefit and assure no loss of any deductible amount as a result of the Internal Revenue Code's percentage and five-year carry-over limitations.[210] Like a conservation easement gift, the contribution of an undivided portion of a person's entire interest in property is an express exception to the rule disallowing deductions for gifts of certain partial interests in property.[211] Unlike the forgiveness of installment obligations as they come due, the periodic donation of undivided interests forces no realization of capital gains. Although the physical subdivision of property followed by the donation of distinct parcels on a periodic basis would accomplish a similar spreading of a deduction that might otherwise be lost, the grant of an undivided interest avoids the cost and complexity of subdividing land, a highly regulated activity in most jurisdictions. To assure that the entire property eventually will go to the conservation organization, a landowner could, by will, devise any portion not donated prior to his death to the conservation organization.

REMAINDER INTEREST

A landowner who wishes to remain in possession of his property during his lifetime, but who, nevertheless, wishes immediately to assure that it will be protected for its conservation values, may reserve a life estate in the property and sell or donate a remainder interest. A life estate entitles a landowner—and anyone else he may designate—to remain in possession of his property during his lifetime, while a remainder interest entitles a grantee organization to receive full ownership of the property upon the death of the last holder of the life estate. Under the usual circumstances, an owner of a life estate will remain liable for the real estate taxes on the property and for all maintenance costs for the duration of his life estate.

The donation of a remainder interest for conservation purposes is deductible as a qualified conservation contribution if it meets the tests for such a contribution under Internal Revenue Code Section 170(h). These are the same tests that a conservation easement must meet in order to be deductible. However, a remainder interest in a personal residence or farm is deductible whether or not it meets the qualified conservation contribution tests.[212]

The donation of a remainder interest is a relatively simple and incontestable substitute for the disposition of property by will. The fact that it offers income as well as estate tax savings makes it doubly attractive as an estate planning device. The valuation of a remainder interest follows actuarial rules that discount the value of the gift for the amount of time the life estate is expected to last.[213] The value of the gift is further reduced by the amount of depreciation of any depreciable improvements on the property that is expected to occur before the life estate expires.[214] The sale or donation of a remainder interest in open space lands provides an excellent means for a landowner to stay on his land, assure its perpetual preservation and at the same time realize some immediate benefit from the appreciation of the property. It is at once an important estate planning and conservation tool.

PURCHASE OPTION, RIGHT OF FIRST REFUSAL AND COVENANT NOT TO SELL

The purchase option, right of first refusal and covenant not to sell are techniques available to conservation organizations and landowners to buy time in the effort to protect environmentally sensitive lands. They can make it possible for a conservation organization to obtain funding for an important purchase with confidence that the land involved will remain available during the term of the option, right or covenant.

A purchase option is a contract, containing all the material elements of a purchase and sale agreement, in which a landowner gives the right to purchase land at a fixed price within a reasonable or stipulated time period or upon the happening of some specified event. The right to purchase creates no obligation; the option binds the landowner but not the person to whom the option is given. Upon exercise of the option, however, its terms become binding on both parties as an agreement for the purchase and sale of land. The exercise of an option relates back to the time when it was given with the result that no person with notice of the option can assert a claim arising after the grant of the option that will be superior to the option. An option supported by consideration is irrevocable, and any consideration received for an option is not taxed until the option is either exercised or expires.

It is unclear under the present tax laws whether, if donated, the fair market value of an option would be a deductible contribution of a partial interest in property. If a donated option were carefully structured to meet the criteria of the qualified conservation contribution section of the Internal Revenue Code, an argument could be made for its deductibility. Under the former qualified conservation contribution section, an option to purchase was explicitly stated to be deductible ("a lease on, option to purchase, or easement with respect to real property granted in perpetuity"—former I.R.C. § 170(f)(3)(B)(iii)). However, the new wording of the same section substitutes a general category: "a restriction (granted in perpetuity) on the uses which may be made of the real property." The Senate Report commenting on this modification states: "This new language would cover easements and other interests in real property that under state property laws have similar attributes (e.g., a restrictive covenant)."[215] Although the Senate Report does not explicitly deny the future deductibility of the gift of an option to purchase, an option to purchase is not, strictly speaking, similar to an easement or a restrictive covenant (although it may include such covenants among its terms) and may, therefore, not be deductible.

In any case, there are practical and legal problems associated with making an option fit the requirements of the conservation contribution deduction. Similar to an executory interest, an option is not considered a vested property interest until it is exercised. If it can be exercised in the too remote future, it may be voidable under the rule against perpetuities just as an executory interest would be.[216] In jurisdictions, including California, where the rule against perpetuities is in force, it may be legally impossible to structure a perpetual option such as the conservation contribution deduction section would require. Any restrictive covenants included in the option terms would not outlast the period of the rule. In addition, an option would fail to protect the conservation values of a property in those situations where only the exercise of the option would suffice to protect them and the option donee is unable for any reason to exercise it. A purchase option simply may not provide the strong assurance of perpetual protection of conservation values that is the guiding principle of the federal conservation deduction legislation. It is a useful temporary conservation technique when a purchase of the optioned land is contemplated in the not too distant future. It is not, however, interchangeable with the conservation easement.

A right of first refusal (also called a preemptive right) resembles an option to purchase but is somewhat more limited. A right of first refusal represents a right to purchase at some future time should a landowner decide to sell. A right of first refusal may be drafted to permit its holder to meet any bona fide offer to purchase the property made by a third party. Alternatively, it may specify all the terms of a sale, including the price, in which case it would operate like an option—to be exercised, if at all, at such time as the owner elected to sell. The latter type, however, may be voidable in the event a specified price is so far below the market value when an owner would like to sell that the right of first refusal would become for all practical purposes a legally impermissible restraint on alienation under Civil Code Section 711.[217]

Finally, as another stopgap measure for preserving environmentally valuable lands, a conservation organization might elicit a covenant from a landowner not to sell a particular property for a certain period of time. A covenant not to sell could be subject to attack as an unreasonable restraint on alienation unless carefully limited in duration and scope.

LEASE

A lease is a contractual arrangement by which a landowner grants the right of possession to his property for a term of years while retaining a reversionary interest allowing him to resume possession when the term expires. A lease to a nonprofit conservation organization might be an effective way to protect lands with conservation values when the conservation organization desires to make some active use of the property and the landowner does not wish to surrender complete control of the property as a whole or of specific rights or uses of the property. A lease for recreational, educational or scientific uses (such as a lease entered into for the purpose of operating a managed nature preserve) may in some situations be the best available approach to providing such uses. A lease may contain covenants restricting the uses of the land for conservation purposes, and both the landowner and the lessee may enforce those covenants as being appurtenant to their interests in the property.

A landowner might, if he were to so choose, donate his reversionary interest to some third-party nonprofit organization, thereby becoming eligible for a deduction for the value of the reversion, or, if the lease were donated as well, for the full value of the land. He also might obtain a deduction while retaining a reversion if the lease granted were in effect perpetual, provided the arrangement met the standards of the federal qualified conservation contribution deduction section.

Although one does not normally think of a lease as the kind of interest that can be granted in perpetuity, there appears to be nothing in our law to prevent the creation of a perpetual lease. California Civil Code Sections 717–718 limit the allowable duration of leases in which rent or services are reserved. Land used for agricultural leases or horticultural purposes cannot be leased for periods longer than fifty-one years; leases of urban property are restricted to a ninety-nine-year period. There is, however, no express restriction on the duration of such leases if no rent or service is reserved. Consequently, the donation of a perpetual lease, or one limited in duration by some remote condition subsequent is theoretically possible.[218] Even if the argument were to be made that a perpetual lease violates the rule against perpetuities—an argument that has been almost universally rejected[219]—perpetuities for charitable purposes are excepted from the operation of that rule.[220]

A lease agreement is a flexible tool for land use and creates a legal relationship between the parties to it that is familiar and well understood by most people. However, use of the lease form should be limited to those situations where the conservation organization involved is prepared to assume primary responsibility for the care of the land in question. Maintenance costs and the duty to pay property taxes, to insure against personal injury liability and to indemnify the landowner against such liability would be likely to be allocated to the conservation organization lessee in a long-term lease arrangement.

One commentator has recommended the lease arrangement to avoid enforceability problems associated with other common law forms such as easements, real covenants, equitable servitudes and defeasible fees.[221] Since conservation easements are enforceable in California, the lease method can be chosen on its own merits—when active possession of the property to be protected is desired—rather than as a cure for the disabilities of other techniques.

TRANSFER IN TRUST

A landowner can assure preservation of the conservation values of his land by transferring the land, or some lesser interest in the land, in trust to a designated trustee instructed to manage it for conservation purposes. The trustee will be held to the highest standard of care in fulfilling his duty of seeing that the landowner's wishes for the property are carried out. The trust may be charitable or noncharitable as the landowner wishes and may be created for a term of years or, if charitable, in perpetuity. A transfer in trust may be made subject to a detailed trust instrument that imposes restrictions on use of the land that the landowner considers appropriate. A trust can be made revocable or irrevocable, amendable or not, as the landowner chooses, depending on how much control of the land he desires to maintain. If the landowner has a complicated scheme in mind for his property and wishes to oversee its use, at least in the beginning, a revocable trust is a useful means for placing the property in the care of another without losing control of it. On the other hand, if the landowner wishes to make a complete gift of his property but nevertheless wants to assure that it be used in some specific way, he can establish an irrevocable trust subject to whatever instructions for its use he wishes followed.

The chief advantage of the trust form is whatever flexibility has been built into it. In the place of some cold legal formulation in a

111

deed, the trust form provides a living trustee, bound to carry out the trust according to the commands of the trust instrument, who is personally charged with perpetuation of the landowner's vision for his property in his management of it.

The trust instrument is the law of the trust. The challenge in drafting it is to define the trust's purposes broadly enough to empower a trustee with sufficient discretion to adapt to changed circumstances on the land without permitting uses contrary to the landowner's intent. An instrument that is drafted too narrowly could cause a trust to lapse if its purpose were to become impossible of fulfillment or, at the least, make judicial intervention necessary to modify the trust. The doctrine of *cy pres* is used by the courts as a means for fulfilling the general charitable intent of charitable trusts if their specific purposes can no longer be carried out. Its application can be avoided—along with the expense and uncertainty that accompany any judicial intervention—if the trust instrument is drafted to provide the trustee with discretion to pursue alternatives to the intended purpose of the trust in the event of the failure of the primary purpose due to changed circumstances.

In a noncharitable trust, the named beneficiary of the trust is the person responsible for its enforcement. In a charitable trust, the public at large is the beneficiary, and, usually, the attorney general of the state in which the property is located is empowered to enforce the trust as the public's representative. In fact, all restricted gifts of land to nonprofit corporations, though not explicitly in trust, are governed by the same rules as charitable gifts made in trust and are subject to the same oversight by the attorney general.

In many states, the supervision of charitable trusts is lax. In California, however, it is taken quite seriously. Charitable corporations and trustees are required to register with the attorney general's office, file their articles of incorporation or other governing instruments and submit periodic written reports concerning their administration of assets held for charitable purposes.[222] The attorney general may investigate the operations of charitable organizations and trusts to assure compliance with their stated charitable purposes.[223] The attorney general may bring suit to enforce a charitable trust, and no court can modify or terminate a charitable trust without making the attorney general a party to the action.[224] A landowner who has chosen to make a gift of land in trust may add to these statutory safeguards by naming a charitable organization as the trust beneficiary or by assigning the power to amend or revoke the trust to a separate conservation organization, thereby interposing an additional entity with an interest in enforcing the trust purposes.[225]

An irrevocable gift of land in trust to a nonprofit organization is a deductible contribution in the same way as an outright fee gift.[226] The restrictions placed on its use merely affect the question of value. A gift of land in trust may be made to a nonprofit organization formed specifically to accept the gift or may be made to an existing conservation organization.

COMMON LAW EASEMENT

Although, in most cases, a conservation easement will be preferable to a common law easement for the protection of conservation values, there are circumstances where, because the requirements for a conservation easement cannot be met, a common law easement might prove an effective conservation tool. The emerging law of conservation easements should provide the basis for the creation of most easements for conservation purposes where nonprofit organizations or governmental entities are to be the holders of the interests created. This will invariably be the case where negative rather than affirmative easements are granted or where affirmative duties, as opposed to rights, are imposed. However, the creation of affirmative rights (e.g., a hiking trail or beach access), along with restrictions designed to preserve the value of those rights, can be efficiently accomplished through the common law easement technique.

An easement is an interest in land of another that entitles its holder to a limited use or enjoyment of the other's land.[227] An easement may be affirmative, allowing the holder to perform specified acts on the subject property (servient tenement), or negative, preventing the owner of the underlying fee from doing a limited number of specified acts. It may be appurtenant, running to the benefit of neighboring land (dominant tenement), or in gross, running to the benefit of a specified individual. Although in many jurisdictions an easement in gross is not transferable, in California an easement in gross is clearly alienable, assignable and inheritable.[228] An easement may be perpetual or of lesser duration according to its terms. Civil Code Sections 801–802 list examples of rights created by easement, both affirmative and negative, appurtenant and in gross. The Code's enumeration is illustrative, not exclusive,[229] and includes a right of way, a right of taking water, wood and minerals, a right of receiving light and air, and a right to the uninterrupted flow of water.

Although the existence of an easement may be implied from circumstances or long-term patterns of use, the express grant of an easement can be accomplished only by a writing that conforms to the requirements for transfer of an interest in real property. The usual method is by deed or by written agreement between the parties to a conveyance. The instrument creating the easement must set forth the essentials of a voluntary conveyance of land by deed: the names of the grantor and grantee, operative words of conveyance, a sufficiently clear description of the easement and the servient tenement, and the grantor's signature.[230] Depending on his requirements, a landowner can grant an easement in his land to another or grant title to his land and reserve an easement to himself.

An express easement may be terminated by release, merger (the holder acquires the servient tenement), prescription (exclusive adverse use by another), estoppel (action by the holder inconsistent with continued existence of the easement), destruction (e.g., of an easement for use of a staircase through a building that is demolished) or intentional abandonment by its holder.[231] Nonuse of the easement is insufficient to show abandonment; there must also be evidence of some act on the part of the easement holder indicating his intent to abandon.[232] In addition, there is authority for the proposition that easements created expressly for a specified purpose terminate when the purpose has been or, for some reason, no longer can be accomplished.[233]

It should be noted that, because they are not qualified under the Conservation Easements Act, federal agencies interested in acquiring easements for conservation purposes in California may have to take care to structure easement transactions in such a way as to avoid the limitations of the common law easement with respect to negative easements, and particularly negative easements in gross.[234] In creating conservation easements, nonprofit conservation organizations and governmental entities on the state, district, county or city level need only concern themselves with the requirements of the Conservation Easements and Open-Space Easement Acts. However, because the Conservation Easements Act is silent regarding the termination of conservation easements, the common law relating to termination will remain important even for these entities.

RESTRICTIVE COVENANTS AND
EQUITABLE SERVITUDES

Restrictive covenants and equitable servitudes (the distinction between them, as will be seen, is purely a legal one) represent yet two more techniques available for accomplishing land conservation purposes. Since the negative easement is such a limited category under the common law, attempts to create such easements are often interpreted as attempts to create restrictive covenants or equitable servitudes and subjected to the tests for validity applicable to those concepts. In California, perhaps the most important characteristic of such restrictions is that they must run to the benefit of particular land.[235] Attempts at creating negative easements in gross cannot, therefore, be saved by interpreting them as restrictive covenants. Only appurtenant negative easements can be so saved. Concern that the typical conservation easement would not fall into either the conventional easement or the restrictive covenant/equitable servitude categories is what made the Conservation Easements Act necessary.

Restrictive covenants and equitable servitudes are binding and enforceable devices for the protection of land where it is clear that they both burden and benefit specific land or interests in land, including easements. They are particularly useful means for restricting land use in a private context, as, for example, between two or more adjoining landowners or among all the landowners in a subdivision. There are, however, several rather technical requirements that must be met before such agreements will be enforced between successors to the covenanting parties.

A covenant is basically an agreement by one party to another to do or not to do a certain thing. A covenant is a promise; it is not, strictly speaking, an interest in real property. However, covenants and equitable servitudes derive their importance from the fact that under certain circumstances they will be interpreted as running with the land concerned and therefore will be enforceable by and against the subsequent owners of such land.

At common law there were four basic requirements for a "running" covenant: (1) the covenant had to be in writing; (2) the original parties to the covenant must have expressed their intent for it to run; (3) the covenant had to "touch and concern" the land, either tangibly (use) or intangibly (affect the estate of a party, e.g., re-move a lien); and (4) a party seeking to enforce the covenant had to be in "privity of estate" with the party against whom he sought to enforce it.[236]

The last requirement was the one on which, historically, most attempts at creating running covenants foundered. In most jurisdic-tions, privity of estate was confined to those persons who held mutual and simultaneous interests in the burdened parcel (e.g., life estate and reversioner, landlord and tenant, or cotenants).[237] In California the strict rule of privity was liberalized for the first time in 1905, when Code Section 1468 was further liberalized to allow for running cov-enants between independent landowners. In 1968 and 1969, Civil Code Section 1468 was further liberalized to allow for running cov-enants between grantors and grantees of land. The cumulative effect of these changes was the elimination of the privity requirement. Section 1468 states the modern California rule: where a covenant "to do or refrain from doing some act" on the covenantor's land "is expressed to be for the benefit of the land of the covenantee," it will run with the land of both parties to bind their successors, if the following requirements are met: (1) the land of the covenantor to be burdened and the land of the covenantee to be benefited must be particularly described in the instrument containing the covenant; (2) successors of the covenantor must be expressly bound for the benefit of the land of the covenantee; (3) the covenant must relate directly to the land; and (4) the instrument containing the covenant must be recorded. Because, under Civil Code Section 1217, unrecorded in-struments are valid between the parties to them and all persons with notice of them, this last requirement should be considered directory rather than mandatory.[238]

The judicial doctrine of equitable servitudes was developed to enable the courts to enforce covenants concerning the use of land that failed to meet the technical requirements for running covenants at law—more often than not, the requirement for privity of estate—but of which the person to be bound had notice. The concept has its principal application in the context of real estate subdivisions, where preservation of the residential character of the development pursuant to a general plan binding all the lots is desired, but simultaneous agreement among all the landowners is, for all practical purposes, impossible. Although developed in the subdivision context, the doc-trine of equitable servitudes is available to save a restriction that does not meet the prerequisites for a running covenant in the two-parcel situation as well. Since the law of restrictive covenants has been liberalized in California, the doctrine of equitable servitudes is, for covenants made after 1969, less important today. It remains viable, however, and will be called into play whenever the Section 1468 requirements have not been met.

Notice of an equitable servitude is necessary for its enforcement. Notice, however, is not sufficient cause for enforcement; mutual agreement must be shown also. The intent of the parties or their predecessors to bind themselves must appear in the chain of title to their lands. Under California case law, the rule governing the creation of valid equitable servitudes in the subdivision context is that reference to the restrictions in question (often set forth at length in a recorded declaration of covenants, conditions and restrictions) must appear in the first covenantor's deed, along with the statement that the restrictions run to the benefit of the remaining lots and are pursuant to a general plan.[239] In addition, the deed must contain a description of the dominant and servient tenements.[240] Although this rule has been criticized, it has been strictly applied to subdivisions in California.[241] It is possible that it could be relaxed in the two-parcel context,[242] but the basic requirements of mutual intent to create a servitude, notice and the appurtenance of both the benefit and burden to specific lands will remain regardless of the context.

Traditionally, an award of damages has been the remedy for breach of a restrictive covenant. In circumstances where damages would prove clearly inadequate to protect the interests involved, however, injunctive relief is usually available. Concern that injunctive relief would not be available for enforcing a restrictive covenant in all situations was another reason for passage of the remedial Conservation Easements Act. It makes the injunction automatically available to enforce conservation restrictions regardless of the form in which they are cast. Injunction is the only remedy for the enenforcement of equitable servitudes.

An important distinction between easements and restrictive covenants/equitable servitudes is the fact that the doctrine of changed conditions is available as a defense to enforcement of the latter. The doctrine of changed conditions provides for the extinguishment of restrictive covenants and equitable servitudes where the character of the restricted property or the surrounding neighborhood has so changed that (1) the restrictions in question no longer

117

serve a viable purpose and (2) it would be oppressive and inequitable to enforce them.[243] It is possible under this rule that local changes affecting the economic value of the restricted property might render restrictions unenforceable, even, conceivably, restrictions with an otherwise still viable conservation purpose. The doctrine of changed conditions allows the courts to substitute their judgment regarding the practicability of a restriction for that of the person interested in its enforcement, making restrictive covenants and equitable servitudes potentially less permanent than easements. Damages still might be available even where a restriction is determined to be unenforceable by way of injunction. An award of damages, however, would be an inadequate remedy for the protection of the conservation values of restricted land.

Under the federal tax legislation, when a landowner places a restrictive covenant on his land he may be eligible for a charitable deduction if the requirements for a qualified conservation contribution under Sections 170(f)(3)(B)(iii) and 170(h) of the Internal Revenue Code are met. The Senate Report states that the general category covering "a restriction (granted in perpetuity) on the use which may be made of real property" embraces easements and other interests in real property that have similar attributes, expressly including, among these, restrictive covenants.[244]

The federal tax legislation, like the California Conservation Easements Act, is not concerned with the technical distinctions between the various common law types of restrictive interests and rights. Along with easements, restrictive covenants and equitable servitudes are deductible when donated to qualified organizations if their effect is to create a perpetual conservation restriction. Their enforceability, however, is hemmed in by the requirements that have been imposed on them through judicial and statutory interpretation. In the case of imperfect restrictive covenants or equitable servitudes, the Conservation Easements Act stands in reserve to bolster such interests in the hands of state, district and local governmental entities and nonprofit conservation organizations. For persons or entities that do not qualify under the Conservation Easements Act, however, the statutory or common law criteria must still be met.

CONCLUSION

The conservation easement is perhaps the most efficient and flexible device available for land conservation today. It is a method of preserving ecologically valuable land that is uniquely designed to match the kind and degree of protection required to the specific characteristics of the land to be protected. Although the costs of monitoring and enforcing conservation easements are not negligible, they are far less than the costs of acquiring and owning land outright. By using conservation easements, communities can benefit from the preservation of more needed open space than would be possible through outright acquisition, without incurring an excessive maintenance burden or removing the land involved from the tax rolls. At the same time, landowners benefit from not having to part with their lands in order to assure their future protection. In addition, they should benefit from the reduction or stabilization of their property taxes and, in the case of a gift, the recoupment, through state and federal tax deductions, of a substantial portion of the development value surrendered.

Although the conservation easement may seem like a novel approach to open space conservation, its roots are deep, and its legal foundation, at least in California, is secure. If care is taken to draft conservation easements thoughtfully, both to meet the criteria of all relevant laws, including the federal tax law, and to provide the clarity necessary to prevent any future confusion as to their reach, the easement technique should prove to be a highly useful and efficient way of preserving the open space our communities need.

This book has dealt with the legal aspects of conservation easements. An understanding of the legal ramifications of these interests is important and necessary for those who use them. However, a basic understanding of the resource values that conservation easements are designed to protect is also an indispensable part of learning to use them well. In addition, negotiating and selling skills are fundamental to the process and must be developed. Knowing the

119

law is one thing, but learning to use it is another. The latter is far more complicated than the former, and experience is the only teacher.

Open space conservation in California is still a new and, for the most part, uncoordinated activity. No full-scale commitment to it has yet been made by the state government, except with regard to the coastal zone. The Open-Space Easement Act and the Conservation Easements Act are tentative steps in the direction of open space protection, but, standing alone, they do not commit the state or local governments to any great degree. They have, however, given those people most committed to land conservation and wise resource use valuable tools for working toward their goals. Nonprofit conservation organizations are being given an opportunity to take the lead in open space protection in California. The job is too big for them alone, of course, but if they show that the easement approach to land conservation can work, help, in the form of greater governmental participation, may not be long in coming.

APPENDIX 1: LEGISLATION

CONSERVATION EASEMENTS ACT OF 1979
(Civ. Code §§ 815-816)

§ 815. Legislative findings and declaration

The Legislature finds and declares that the preservation of land in its natural, scenic, agricultural, historical, forested, or open-space condition is among the most important environmental assets of California. The Legislature further finds and declares it to be the public policy and in the public interest of this state to encourage the voluntary conveyance of conservation easements to qualified nonprofit organizations.

§ 815.1. Conservation easement

For the purposes of this chapter, "conservation easement" means any limitation in a deed, will, or other instrument in the form of an easement, restriction, covenant, or condition, which is or has been executed by or on behalf of the owner of the land subject to such easement and is binding upon successive owners of such land, and the purpose of which is to retain land predominantly in its natural, scenic, historical, agricultural, forested, or open-space condition.

§ 815.2. Nature

(a) A conservation easement is an interest in real property voluntarily created and freely transferable in whole or in part for the purposes stated in Section 815.1 by any lawful method for the transfer of interests in real property in this state.

(b) A conservation easement shall be perpetual in duration.

(c) A conservation easement shall not be deemed personal in nature and shall constitute an interest in real property notwithstanding the fact that it may be negative in character.

(d) The particular characteristics of a conservation easement shall be those granted or specified in the instrument creating or transferring the easement.

§ 815.3. Entities authorized to acquire and hold conservation easements

Only the following entities or organizations may acquire and hold conservation easements:

(a) Tax-exempt nonprofit organization qualified under Section 501(c)(3) of the Internal Revenue Code and qualified to do business in this state which has as its primary purpose the preservation, protection, or enhancement of land in its natural, scenic, historical, agricultural, forested, or open-space condition or use.

(b) The state or any city, county, city and county, district, or other state or local governmental entity, if otherwise authorized to acquire and hold title to real property and if the conservation easement is voluntarily conveyed. No local governmental entity may condition the issuance of an entitlement for use on the applicant's granting of a conservation easement pursuant to this chapter.

§ 815.4. Reservation of interests in grantor

All interests not transferred and conveyed by the instrument creating the easement shall remain in the grantor of the easement, including the right to engage in all uses of the land not affected by the easement nor prohibited by the easement or by law.

§ 815.5. Recordation

Instruments creating, assigning, or otherwise transferring conservation easements shall be recorded in the office of the county recorder of the county where the land is situated, in whole or in part, and such instruments shall be subject in all respects to the recording laws.

§ 815.7. Enforcement of easement; injunctive relief; damages; costs

(a) No conservation easement shall be unenforceable by reason of lack of privity of contract or lack of benefit to particular land or because not expressed in the instrument creating it as running with the land.

(b) Actual or threatened injury to or impairment of a conservation easement or actual or threatened violation of its terms may be prohibited or restrained, or the interest intended for protection by such easement may be enforced, by injunctive relief granted by any court of competent jurisdiction in a proceeding initiated by the grantor or by the owner of the easement.

(c) In addition to the remedy of injunctive relief, the holder of a conservation easement shall be entitled to recover money damages for any injury to such easement or to the interest being protected thereby or for the violation of the terms of such easement. In assessing such damages there may be taken into account, in addition to the cost of restoration and other usual rules of the law of damages, the loss of scenic, aesthetic, or environmental value to the real property subject to the easement.

(d) The court may award to the prevailing party in any action authorized by this section the costs of litigation, including reasonable attorney's fees.

§ 815.9. Political subdivisions; authority to hold comparable easements

Nothing in this chapter shall be construed to impair or conflict with the operation of any law or statute conferring upon any political subdivision the right or power to hold interests in land comparable to conservation easements, including, but not limited to, Chapter 12 (commencing with Section 6950) of Division 7 of Title 1 of, Chapter 6.5 (commencing with Section 51050), Chapter 6.6 (commencing with Section 51070) and Chapter 7 (commencing with Section 51200) of Part 1 of Division 1 of Title 5 of, and Article 10.5 (commencing with Section 65560) of Chapter 3 of Title 7 of, the Government Code, and Article 1.5 (commencing with Section 421) of Chapter 3 of Part 2 of Division 1 of the Revenue and Taxation Code.

§ 816. Liberal construction of chapter

The provisions of this chapter shall be liberally construed in order to effectuate the policy and purpose of Section 815.

OPEN-SPACE EASEMENT ACT OF 1974
(Gov't Code §§ 51070-51097)

ARTICLE 1. DECLARATION

§ 51070. Legislative intent

It is the intent of the Legislature in enacting this chapter to provide a means whereby any county or city may acquire or approve an open-space easement in perpetuity or for a term of years for the purpose of preserving and maintaining open space.

§ 51071. Legislative findings

The Legislature finds that the rapid growth and spread of urban development is encroaching upon, or eliminating open-space lands which are necessary not only for the maintenance of the economy of the state, but also for the assurance of the continued availability of land for the production of food and fiber, for the enjoyment of scenic beauty, for recreation and for the use and conservation of natural resources.

§ 51072. Legislative declaration

The Legislature hereby declares that open-space lands, if preserved and maintained, would constitute important physical, social, economic or aesthetic assets to existing or pending urban development.

§ 51073. Additional legislative declaration

The Legislature further declares that the acquisition of open-space easements is in the public interest and constitutes a public purpose for which public funds may be expended or advanced.

ARTICLE 2. DEFINITIONS

§ 51075. Definitions

As used in this chapter, unless otherwise apparent from the context:

(a) "Open-space land" means any parcel or area of land or water which is essentially unimproved and devoted to an open-space use as defined in Section 65560 of the Government Code.

(b) "City" means any city or city and county.

(c) "Landowner" includes a lessee or trustee, if the expiration of the lease or trust occurs at a time later than the expiration of the open-space restriction or any extension thereof.

(d) "Open-space easement" means any right or interest in perpetuity or for a term of years in open-space land acquired by a county, city, or nonprofit organization pursuant to this chapter where the deed or other instrument granting such right or interest imposes restrictions which, through limitation of future use, will effectively preserve for public use or enjoyment the natural or scenic character of such open-space land. An open-space easement shall contain a covenant with the county, city, or nonprofit organization running with the land, either in perpetuity or for a term of years, that the land-owner shall not construct or permit the construction of improvements except those for which the right is expressly reserved in the instrument provided that such reservation would not be inconsistent with the purposes of this chapter and which would not be incompatible with maintaining and preserving the natural or scenic character of the land. Any such covenant shall not prohibit the construction of either public service facilities installed for the benefit of the land subject to such covenant or public service facilities installed pursuant to an authorization by the governing body of the county or city or the Public Utilities Commission.

(e) "Open-space plan" means the open-space element of a county or city general plan adopted by the local governing body pursuant to Section 65560 of the Government Code.

(f) "Nonprofit organization" means any organization qualifying under Section 501(c)(3) of the Internal Revenue Code in the preceding tax year, and which includes the preservation of open space as a stated purpose in its articles of incorporation. Such qualification shall be demonstrated by a letter of determination from the Internal Revenue Service.

ARTICLE 3. GENERAL PROVISIONS

§ 51080. Counties or cities authorized to accept or approve grants

Any county or city which has an adopted open-space plan may accept or approve a grant of an open-space easement on privately owned lands lying within the county or city in the manner provided in this chapter.

§ 51081. Execution and acceptance; dedication to public; minimum term; automatic extension of one year on anniversary date of acceptance

The execution and acceptance of a deed or other instrument described in subdivision (d) of Section 51075 shall constitute a dedication to the public of the open-space character of the lands for the term specified. Any such easement and covenant shall run for a term of not less than 10 years. An open-space easement for a term of years shall provide that on the anniversary date of the acceptance of the open-space easement or on such other annual date as specified by the deed or other instrument described in subdivision (d) of Section

51075, a year shall be added automatically to the initial term unless a notice of nonrenewal is given as provided in Section 51091.

§ 51082. Restrictions, conditions or covenants in deed or conveyance; requirement by city or county

A county or city may require a deed or other instrument described in subdivision (d) of Section 51075 to contain any such restrictions, conditions or covenants as are necessary or desirable to maintain the natural or scenic character of the land or to prevent any activity, use or action which could impair the open-space character of the land.

§ 51083. Resolution of acceptance or approval; endorsement on deed or other instrument

No deed or other instrument described in subdivision (d) of Section 51075 shall be effective until it has been accepted or approved by resolution of the governing body of the county or city and its acceptance endorsed thereon.

§ 51083.5. Acceptance of easement by nonprofit organization; approval by county or city

Notwithstanding any provisions of this chapter, the grant of any easement to a nonprofit organization shall be effective upon its acceptance by such organization. However, for the purposes of this chapter and Sections 421 to 432, inclusive, of the Revenue and Taxation Code, no such easement shall be considered as granted pursuant to this chapter unless the grant of such easement has been approved by the county or city in which the land lies pursuant to the provisions of this article.

§ 51084. Resolution of findings; necessity for acceptance and approval

No grant of an open-space easement shall be accepted or approved by a county or city, unless the governing body, by resolution, finds:

(a) That the preservation of the land as open space is consistent with the general plan of the county and city; and

(b) That the preservation of the land as open space is in the best interest of the county or city and specifically because one or more of the following reasons exist:

(1) That the land is essentially unimproved and if retained in its natural state has either scenic value to the public, or is valuable as a watershed or as a wildlife preserve, and the instrument contains appropriate covenants to that end.

(2) It is in the public interest that the land be retained as open space because such land either will add to the amenities of living in neighboring urbanized areas or will help preserve the rural character of the area in which the land is located.

(3) The public interest will otherwise be served in a manner recited in the resolution and consistent with the purposes of this subdivision and Section 8 of Article XIII of the Constitution of the State of California.

The resolution of the governing body shall establish a conclusive presumption that the conditions set forth in subdivisions (a) and (b) have been satisfied.

§ 51085. Report of planning department or commission

The governing body of the county or city may not accept or approve any grant of an open-space easement until the matter has first been referred to the county or city planning department or planning commission and a report thereon has been received from the planning department or planning commission. Within 30 days after receiving the proposal to accept or approve a grant of an open-space easement, the planning department or planning commission shall submit its report to the governing body. The governing body may extend the time for submitting such a report for an additional period not exceeding 30 days. The report shall specify whether the proposal is consistent with the general plan of the jurisdiction.

§ 51086. Prohibition of building permit on land with open-space easement; injunction by county, city, private person or nonprofit organization; right of eminent domain

(a) From and after the time when an open-space easement has been accepted or approved by the county or city and its acceptance or approval endorsed thereon, no building permit may be issued for any structure which would violate the easement and the county or city shall seek by appropriate proceedings an injunction against any threatened construction or other development or activity on the land which would violate the easement and shall seek a mandatory injunction requiring the removal of any structure erected in violation of the easement.

In the event the county or city fails to seek an injunction against any threatened construction or other development or activity on the land which would violate the easement or to seek a mandatory injunction requiring the removal of any structure erected in violation of the easement, or if the county or city should construct any structure or development or conduct or permit any activity in violation of the easement, the owner of any property within the county or city, or any resident thereof, may, by appropriate proceedings, seek such an injunction.

(b) In the case of an open-space easement granted to a nonprofit organization pursuant to this chapter, such organization shall seek, through its official representatives, an injunction against any threatened construction or other development or activity on the land which would violate the easement and shall seek a mandatory injunction requiring the removal of any structure erected in violation of the easement.

(c) The court may award to a plaintiff or defendant who prevails in an action authorized by this section his or her costs of litigation, including reasonable attorney's fees.

(d) Nothing in this chapter shall limit the power of the state, or any department or agency thereof, or any county, city, school district, or any other local public district, agency or entity, or any other person authorized by law, to acquire land subject to an open-space easement by eminent domain.

§ 51087. Recordation and filing; notice

Upon the acceptance or approval of any instrument creating an open-space easement the clerk of the governing body shall record the same in the office of the county recorder and file a copy thereof with the county assessor. From and after the time of such recordation such easement shall impart such notice thereof to all persons as is afforded by the recording laws of this state.

ARTICLE 4. TERMINATION OF AN OPEN-SPACE EASEMENT

§ 51090. Methods

An open-space easement for a term of years may be terminated only in accordance with the provisions of this article. An open-space easement may be terminated only by:

(a) Nonrenewal, or

(b) Abandonment.

Abandonment of an easement granted to the county or city pursuant to this chapter shall be controlled by Section 51093.

Abandonment or nonrenewal of an easement granted to a non-profit organization pursuant to this chapter shall be effective only if approved by appropriate resolution of the governing body of such organization and such abandonment or nonrenewal initiated by a nonprofit organization has been approved by the county or city in which the land lies in the manner provided in Section 51093.

§ 51091. Notice of nonrenewal; service; protest by owner

If either the landowner or the county, city, or nonprofit organization desires in any year not to renew the open-space easement, that party shall serve written notice of nonrenewal of the easement upon the other party at least 90 days in advance of the annual renewal date of the open-space easement. Unless such written notice is served at least 90 days in advance of the renewal date, the open-space easement shall be considered renewed as provided in Section 51081.

Upon receipt by the owner of a notice from the county, city, or nonprofit organization of nonrenewal, the owner may make a written protest of the notice of nonrenewal. The county, city, or nonprofit organization may, at any time prior to the renewal date, withdraw the notice of nonrenewal.

§ 51092. Length of continuance after notice of intent of nonrenewal

If the county, city, or nonprofit organization or the landowner serves notice of intent in any year not to renew the open-space easement, the existing open-space easement shall remain in effect for the balance of the period remaining since the original execution or the last renewal of the open-space easement, as the case may be.

§ 51093. Petition to governing body for abandonment; approval by resolution; findings and other conditions; fee

(a) The landowner may petition the governing body of the county or city for abandonment of any open-space easement or in the case of an open-space easement granted to a nonprofit organization pursuant to this chapter, for approval of abandonment by such organization, as to all of the subject land. The governing body may approve the abandonment of an open-space easement only if, by resolution, it finds:

(1) That no public purpose described in Section 51084 will be served by keeping the land as open space; and

(2) That the abandonment is not inconsistent with the purposes of this chapter; and

(3) That the abandonment is consistent with the local general plan; and

(4) That the abandonment is necessary to avoid a substantial financial hardship to the landowner due to involuntary factors unique to him.

No resolution abandoning an open-space easement, or approving the abandonment of an open-space easement granted to a nonprofit organization pursuant to this chapter, shall be finally adopted until the matter has been referred to the county or city planning commission, the commission has held a public hearing thereon and furnished a report on the matter to the governing body stating whether the abandonment is consistent with the local general plan and the governing body has held at least one public hearing thereon after giving 30 days' notice thereof by publication in accordance with Section 6061 of the Government Code, and by posting notice on the land.

(b) Prior to approval of the resolution abandoning or approving the abandonment of an open-space easement, the county assessor of the county in which the land subject to the open-space easement is located shall determine the full cash value of the land as though it were free of the open-space easement. The assessor shall multiply such value by 25 percent, and shall certify the product to the governing body as the abandonment valuation of the land for the purpose of determining the abandonment fee.

(c) Prior to giving approval to the abandonment of any open-space easement, the governing body shall determine and certify to the county auditor the amount of the abandonment fee which the landowner must pay the county treasurer upon abandonment. That fee shall be an amount equal to 50 percent of the abandonment valuation of the property.

(d) Any sum collected pursuant to this section shall be transmitted by the county treasurer to the State Controller and be deposited in the State General Fund.

(e) An abandonment shall not become effective until the abandonment fee has been paid in full.

§ 51094. Recordation of certified copy of resolution of abandonment

Upon the recording in the office of the county recorder of a certified copy of a resolution abandoning or approving the abandonment of an open-space easement and reciting compliance with the provisions of Section 51093, the land subject thereto shall be deemed relieved of the easement and the covenants of the owner contained therein shall be deemed terminated; provided, however, that no certified copy of any resolution abandoning or approving the abandonment of an open-space easement shall be recorded until the abandonment fee has been paid in full.

ARTICLE 5. EMINENT DOMAIN AND OTHER PROVISIONS

§ 51095. Termination of easement at time of filing of complaint in condemnation; right of compensation

If any land or a portion thereof as to which any city or county has accepted or approved an open-space easement pursuant to this chapter is thereafter sought to be condemned for public use and the easement was received as a gift without the payment of any compensation therefor, the easement shall terminate as of the time of the filing of the complaint in condemnation as to the land or portion thereof sought to be taken for public use, and the owner shall be entitled to such compensation for the taking as he would have been entitled to had the land not been burdened by the easement.

§ 51096. Open-space easement deemed enforceable restriction

Lands subject to the grant of an open-space easement executed and accepted in accordance with this chapter shall be deemed to be enforceably restricted within the meaning of Section 8 of Article XIII of the Constitution of the State of California.

§ 51097. Right or power of city or county to purchase or acquire property to preserve open space

Nothing in this chapter shall be deemed to prevent or restrict the right or power of any county or city to acquire by purchase, gift, grant, bequest, devise, lease or otherwise any right or interest in real property for the purpose of preserving open space or for any other purpose under any other provisions of law.

FEDERAL TAX DEDUCTION:
TAX TREATMENT EXTENSION ACT OF 1980
(I.R.C. §§ 170(f)(3) and 170(h))

§ **170(f)(3) Denial of deduction in case of certain contributions of partial interests in property.—**

(A) **In general.**—In the case of a contribution (not made by a transfer in trust) of an interest in property which consists of less than the taxpayer's entire interest in such property, a deduction shall be allowed under this section only to the extent that the value of the interest contributed would be allowable as a deduction under this section if such interest had been transferred in trust. For purposes of this subparagraph, a contribution by a taxpayer of the right to use property shall be treated as a contribution of less than the taxpayer's entire interest in such property.

(B) **Exceptions.**—Subparagraph (A) shall not apply to—

(i)　a contribution of a remainder interest in a personal residence or farm,

(ii) a contribution of an undivided portion of the taxpayer's entire interest in property, and

(iii) a qualified conservation contribution.

§ **170(h) Qualified conservation contribution.—**

(1) **In general.**—For purposes of subsection (f)(3)(B)(iii), the term "qualified conservation contribution" means a contribution—

(A) of a qualified real property interest,

(B) to a qualified organization,

(C) exclusively for conservation purposes.

(2) **Qualified real property interest.**—For purposes of this subsection, the term "qualified real property interest" means any of the following interests in real property:

(A) the entire interest of the donor other than a qualified mineral interest,

(B) a remainder interest, and

(C) a restriction (granted in perpetuity) on the use which may be made of the real property.

(3) **Qualified organization.**—For purposes of paragraph (1), the term "qualified organization" means an organization which—

(A) is described in clause (v) or (vi) of subsection (b)(1)(A),
or

(B) is described in section 501(c)(3) and—

(i) meets the requirements of section 509(a)(2), or

(ii) meets the requirements of section 509(a)(3) and is controlled by an organization described in subparagraph (A) or in clause (i) of this subparagraph.

(4) **Conservation purpose defined.**—

(A) **In general.**—For purposes of this subsection, the term "conservation purpose" means—

(i) the preservation of land areas for outdoor recreation by, or the education of, the general public,

(ii) the protection of a relatively natural habitat of fish, wildlife, or plants, or similar ecosystem,

(iii) the preservation of open space (including farmland and forest land) where such preservation is—

(I) for the scenic enjoyment of the general public, or

(II) pursuant to clearly delineated Federal, State, or local governmental conservation policy,

and will yield a significant public benefit, or

(iv) the preservation of an historically important land area or a certified historic structure.

(B) **Certified historic structure.**—For purposes of subparagraph (A)(iv), the term "certified historic structure" means any building, structure, or land area which—

(i) is listed in the National Register, or

(ii) is located in a registered historic district (as defined in section 191(d)(2)) and is certified by the Secretary of the Interior to the Secretary as being of historic significance to the district.

A building, structure, or land area satisfies the preceding sentence if it satisfies such sentence either at the time of the transfer or on the due date (including extensions) for filing the transferor's return under this chapter for the taxable year in which the transfer is made.

(5) **Exclusively for conservation purposes.**—For purposes of this subsection—

(A) **Conservation purpose must be protected.**—A contribution shall not be treated as exclusively for conservation purposes unless the conservation purpose is protected in perpetuity.

(**B**) **No surface mining permitted.**—In the case of a contribution of any interest where there is a retention of a qualified mineral interest, subparagraph (A) shall not be treated as met if at any time there may be extraction or removal of minerals by any surface mining method.

(**6**) **Qualified mineral interest.**—For purposes of this subsection, the term "qualified mineral interest" means—

(A) subsurface oil, gas, or other minerals, and

(B) the right to access to such minerals.

APPENDIX 2:
SAMPLE CONSERVATION EASEMENT

Note: This rather generalized sample easement is the product of a review of numerous conservation easements obtained from many different sources. It is offered more as an illustration than a model. Because the particular circumstances of individual easement transactions are so various, and the importance of customizing the easement document to conform to the circumstances at hand is so great, all that should be expected of a sample of this type is that it suggest an approach and provide some organizational guidance. This sample is meant to serve, in conjunction with the checklist in Chapter Three, as an aid in dealing with some of the problems involved in drafting an easement. It should not, however, be used as a substitute for thinking through those problems on a case-by-case basis.

This sample easement is predicated on a hypothetical, large rural farm/ranch assumed to contain significant scenic and some natural conservation features, including wildlife habitat and wetlands. It is drafted with the requirements of the California Easements Act (Civ. Code §§ 815–816) and Internal Revenue Code Sections 170(f)(3)(B) and (h) in mind. If some other legislation, such as the Open-Space Easement Act, were involved, it would be necessary to modify the terms of the easement document to reflect the particular requirements of the legislation in question.

DEED OF CONSERVATION EASEMENT

THIS GRANT DEED OF CONSERVATION EASEMENT is made this _____ day of _____, 198____, by _____ and _____ _____, husband and wife, having an address at _____ _____ ("Grantors"), in favor of _____ _____, a nonprofit California corporation having an address at _____ _____ ("Grantee").

WITNESSETH:

WHEREAS, Grantors are the owners of certain real property ("the Property") in _____ County, California, more particularly described in Exhibit A attached hereto and incorporated herein by this reference; and

WHEREAS, the Property is in a substantially undisturbed natural and open space condition and exhibits natural, scenic and open space features of great importance to Grantors, the people of the region and the people of the State of California, and in particular _____[Describe any exceptional features]_____ ; and

WHEREAS, protection of the natural, scenic and open space values of the Property will help to sustain the ecological integrity of the region and the plant and wildlife dependent on it; and

WHEREAS, the specific natural, scenic, open space and ecological values of the Property are documented in the ecological survey made by Grantee and dated _____, 198__, which survey, to be kept current by Grantee, will serve as an information base line for monitoring compliance with the terms of this grant; and

WHEREAS, Grantors desire and intend that the natural, scenic, open space and ecological values of the Property be preserved and maintained by the continuation of land use patterns on the Property, such as those involved in farming and ranching, that will not significantly impair or interfere with those values; and

WHEREAS, Grantors, as owners in fee of the Property, own the affirmative rights to identify and preserve the natural, scenic, open space and ecological values of the Property; and

WHEREAS, Grantors desire and intend to transfer those rights to Grantee in perpetuity; and

WHEREAS, Grantee is a publicly supported, tax-exempt nonprofit organization, qualified under Section 501(c)(3) of the Internal Revenue Code, whose primary purpose is the preservation, protection or enhancement of land in its natural, scenic, historical, agricultural, forested or open space condition; and

WHEREAS, Grantee agrees by accepting this grant to honor and defend the intentions of Grantors stated herein and to preserve and protect in perpetuity the natural, scenic, open space and ecological values of the Property for the benefit of this generation and the generations to come;

NOW, THEREFORE, in consideration of the facts recited above and the mutual covenants, terms, conditions and restrictions contained herein, and pursuant to Sections 815 and 816 of the California Civil Code, Grantors hereby voluntarily grant and convey to Grantee a conservation easement in perpetuity over the Property of the nature and character and to the extent hereinafter set forth.

1. It is the purpose of this conservation easement to assure that the Property will be retained forever predominantly in its natural, scenic and open space condition and to prevent any use of the Property that will significantly impair or interfere with the natural, scenic, open space and ecological values of the Property. To carry out this purpose the following rights are conveyed to Grantee by this easement:

(a) To identify, preserve, protect and, in consultation with Grantors, enhance the natural, scenic, open space and ecological features of the Property, including, without limitation, topography, soil, water, vegetation and wildlife;

(b) To enter upon the Property at reasonable times to enforce the rights herein granted and to observe, study and make scientific observations of the Property, upon prior notice to Grantors, their heirs, successors or assigns, in a manner that will not unreasonably interfere with the use and quiet enjoyment of the Property by Grantors, their heirs, successors or assigns at the time of such entry;

(c) To enjoin any activity on or use of the Property that is inconsistent with the purpose of this conservation easement and to enforce the restoration of such areas or features of the Property that may be damaged by any inconsistent activity or use.

2. Grantors intend that this conservation easement will confine the use of the Property to activities such as farming, ranching and ecological study that are consistent with the purpose of this conservation easement.

2.1 Grantors state that the following uses and practices, though not an exhaustive recital of consistent uses and practices, are *consistent* with Grantors' intent and the purpose of this conservation easement and are not precluded, prevented or limited by it:

(a) To raise, pasture and graze livestock of every

nature and description and to plant, raise and harvest agricultural crops of every nature and description by the use of sound economic ranching and agricultural practices, including the prudent use of fertilizers and such pesticides, herbicides, insecticides, fungicides or other techniques for the control of insects, weeds, diseases and pests that are necessary to maintain the productivity of the croplands or rangelands; provided, however, that in no case will such ranching and agricultural activities be permitted to result in overgrazing or in the pollution of any surface or subsurface waters or otherwise contribute to the substantial degradation or impairment of the natural, scenic, open space or ecological features of the Property;

(b) To develop and maintain those water resources on the Property that are necessary for permitted ranching, agricultural and domestic purposes;

(c) To maintain and, in an unobtrusive manner, en-large existing ranching, agricultural, residential and related struc-tures and improvements and, in the event of their destruction, to replace them with similarly situated structures or facilities of like size, function and capacity;

(d) To construct, in consultation with Grantee, such additional improvements for ranching and agricultural purposes that do not significantly impair or interfere with the natural, scenic, open space and ecological values of the Property;

(e) To construct, in consultation with Grantee, three (3) additional residential structures and related improvements for Grantors, their heirs, successors, assigns or employees in the loca-tions described as follows: [description]   .

(f) To bury or otherwise camouflage all utility systems or extensions of existing utility systems constructed in the future;

(g) To control predatory and problem animals, but only through the use of selective techniques that are limited in their effect to the specific animal or animals that have caused significant damage to livestock or other property; and

(h) To fish and hunt waterfowl and game animals at levels not detrimental to maintaining the optimum balance of fish and wildlife within the available habitat.

2.2 Grantors state that the following uses and practices, though not an exhaustive recital of inconsistent uses and practices, are *inconsistent* with Grantors' intent and the purpose of this conservation easement and are, therefore, prohibited by it:

(a) The legal or *de facto* subdivision of the Property for any purpose;

(b) Any commercial or industrial use of or activity on the Property other than permitted ranching or farming uses and activities;

(c) The construction of any buildings, structures or other improvements except as permitted under section 2.1;

(d) The establishment or maintenance of any feed lot;

(e) The exploration for or extraction of minerals, hydrocarbons, soils or other materials on or below the surface of the Property;

(f) The dumping or other disposal of noncompostible refuse on the Property except at sites approved by Grantee;

(g) Any use or activity that causes or presents a substantial risk of causing soil erosion;

(h) The cutting of live trees other than on a sustained yield basis in accordance with a plan approved by Grantee that is designed to protect the natural, scenic, open space and ecological values of the Property or except as necessary to control or prevent imminent hazard, disease or fire or to restore natural habitat areas or promote native vegetation;

(i) The alteration or manipulation of the ponds and water courses located on the Property, or the removal of water therefrom, except as necessary for permitted ranching, agricultural and domestic purposes;

(j) The construction, maintenance or erection of any signs or billboards on the Property;

(k) The use of off-road vehicles, except in emergencies, in any manner or location that is likely to result in significant soil erosion or compaction or significant adverse impact on vegetation or wildlife; and

(l) The filling, dredging or diking of wetland areas.

3. Grantors reserve to themselves, their heirs, successors or assigns all rights as owners of the Property, including the right to engage in all uses of the Property that are not expressly prohibited herein and are not inconsistent with the purpose of this conservation easement.

4. No right of access by the general public to any portion of the Property is conveyed by this conservation easement.

5. Grantors agree to bear all costs and liabilities of any kind related to the operation, upkeep and maintenance of the Property and do hereby indemnify and hold Grantee harmless therefrom.

6. Grantors agree to pay any and all real property taxes and assessments levied by competent authority on the Property.

7. Grantee agrees to pay all costs associated with its obligation to honor and defend the intentions of Grantors stated herein and to preserve and protect in perpetuity the natural, scenic, open space and ecological values of the Property, including any costs incurred in monitoring compliance with the terms of this conservation easement; however, Grantors intend that any costs incurred by Grantee in enforcing, judicially or otherwise, the terms and restrictions of this conservation easement against Grantors, their heirs, successors, personal representatives or assigns, including, without limitation, costs of suit, attorneys' fees and any costs of restoration necessitated by the violation of the terms of this conservation easement by Grantors, their heirs, successors, personal representatives or assigns, shall be borne by Grantors, their heirs, successors, personal representatives or assigns.

8. Grantors intend that enforcement of the terms and provisions of the conservation easement shall be at the discretion of Grantee and that any forebearance on behalf of Grantee to exercise its rights hereunder in the event of any breach hereof by Grantors, their heirs, successors, personal representatives or assigns shall not be deemed or construed to be a waiver of Grantee's rights hereunder in the event of any subsequent breach.

9. Grantee agrees that it will hold this conservation easement exclusively for conservation purposes and that it will not assign its rights and obligations under this conservation easement except to another organization qualified to hold such interests under the applicable state and federal laws and committed to holding this conservation easement exclusively for conservation purposes.

10. If any provision of this conservation easement or the application thereof to any person or circumstance is found to be invalid, the remainder of the provisions of this conservation easement, and the application of such provision to persons or circumstances

other than those as to which it is found to be invalid, shall not be affected thereby.

11. All notices, consents, approvals or other communications hereunder shall be in writing and shall be deemed properly given if sent by United States certified mail, return receipt requested, addressed to the appropriate party or successor in interest.

12. Grantors agree that the terms, conditions, restrictions and purposes of this grant will be inserted by them in any subsequent deed or other legal instrument by which Grantors divest themselves of any interest in the Property.

TO HAVE AND TO HOLD unto Grantee, its successors and assigns forever. The covenants, terms, conditions, restrictions and purposes imposed with this grant shall not only be binding upon Grantors but also their agents, personal representatives, heirs, assigns and all other successors to them in interest, and shall continue as a servitude running in perpetuity with the Property.

IN WITNESS WHEREOF Grantors have set their hands on the day and year first above written.

_____

_____

Grantors

ACCEPTED:

_____

_____

Grantee

[Acknowledgment]

NOTES

1. *See generally* FARMLANDS CONSERVATION PROJECT OF PEOPLE FOR OPEN SPACE, ENDANGERED HARVEST: THE FUTURE OF BAY AREA FARMLAND (Nov. 1980).

2. *See* REPORT BY THE COMPTROLLER GEN. OF THE U.S. TO THE SUBCOMM. ON NAT'L PARKS & INSULAR AFFAIRS, HOUSE COMM. ON INTERIOR & INSULAR AFFAIRS, THE FEDERAL DRIVE TO ACQUIRE PRIVATE LANDS SHOULD BE REASSESSED 24–25 (Dec. 14, 1979) (recommending wider use of alternatives, including easements, to outright purchase of lands by federal government); *see also* WHYTE, THE LAST LANDSCAPE 93 (1968).

3. THE FEDERAL DRIVE TO ACQUIRE PRIVATE LANDS, *supra* note 2.

4. 779 Stat. 1028, 23 U.S.C. §§ 131, 136, 319.

5. Pursuant to Title VII of the Housing Act of 1961, 42 U.S.C. §§ 1500–1500d-1.

6. WHYTE, *supra* note 2, at 93–94.

7. *See* SUTTE & CUNNINGHAM, NATIONAL COOP. HIGHWAY RESEARCH PROGRAM, REPORT NO. 56, SCENIC EASEMENTS: LEGAL, ADMINISTRATIVE AND VALUATION PROBLEMS AND PROCEDURES 22–23 (1968). The authority to purchase or condemn easements and other interests in real property is granted at CAL. PUB. RES. CODE § 5006.

8. *See, e.g.,* CAL. GOV'T CODE §§ 7000–7001 (easements adjacent to I-5) and CAL. STS. & HY. CODE §§ 895–897 (contingent on availability of federal funds).

9. *See* Federal Tax Benefits and Land Conservation (K. Browne ed. 1979) (transcript of meeting sponsored by Brandywine Conservancy on Sept. 29, 1979, at Chadds Ford, Pennsylvania).

10. In addition to The Trust for Public Land, The Nature Conservancy is likely to be a good source of practical knowledge concerning use of the easement technique. The Conservancy holds numerous conservation easements in all parts of the country, including easements covering 74,000 acres in Adirondack Park in New York State. *See* The Nature Conservancy News Vol. 30, No. 5, at 5, 19–22 (1980). Among the Conservancy's holdings in California is a conservation easement over Santa Cruz Island in the ecologically critical Channel Island group off the coast of Santa Barbara. Still another

important source of information and assistance will be the State Coastal Conservancy, which is developing considerable expertise in this area while actively soliciting and subsidizing local land trust participation in its programs.

11. 1955 Cal. Stat., ch. 1712, § 1, at 3147.

12. Note, *Preservation of Open Spaces Through Scenic Easements and Greenbelt Zoning*, 12 STAN. L. REV. 638 (1960).

13. CALIFORNIA LEGISLATURE, JOINT COMMITTEE ON OPEN SPACE LANDS PRELIMINARY REPORT 28 (Mar. 1969) (hereafter referred to as PRELIMINARY REPORT).

14. *Id.*

15. SB 1461 (Farr), Stats. 1959, ch. 1658, § 1, at 4035, CAL. GOV'T CODE §§ 6950–6954.

16. Senator Farr (author, SB 1461), Letter to Governor Edmund G. Brown (June 23, 1959).

17. Whyte, *Securing Open Space for Urban America*, URB. LAND INST. TECH. BULL. 55, No. 36 (1959).

18. *See* PRELIMINARY REPORT, *supra* note 13, at 29.

19. *Id.*

20. *Id.* at 23.

21. *Id.* at 29–32.

22. AB 2117 (Williamson), Stats 1965, ch. 1443, § 1, at 3377, CAL. GOV'T CODE §§ 51200–51295.

23. PRELIMINARY REPORT, *supra* note 13, at 11.

24. Now art. XIII, § 8. *See* pp. 36–37.

25. Sections 421–425 were amended first in 1969 and then in later years to reflect the recommendations of the Joint Committee on Open Space Land as well as subsequent legislation. The present §§ 421–430.5 are discussed more fully at pp. 73–75.

26. PRELIMINARY REPORT, *supra* note 13, at 11.

27. STATE OF CAL. DEP'T OF FIN., A REVIEW OF THE CALIFORNIA LAND CONSERVATION ACT 3–4, REPORT NO. 580-8 (Oct. 1980).

28. *See* Currier, *An Analysis of Differential Taxation as a Method of Maintaining Agricultural and Open Space Land Uses*, 11 LAND USE & ENV'T L. REV. 443, 458–459 (1980).

29. *Id.* at 457.

30. PRELIMINARY REPORT, *supra* note 13, at 23.

31. AB 1176 (Knox), Stats 1969, ch. 762, § 1, at 1521, CAL. GOV'T CODE §§ 51050–51065.

32. LEGISLATIVE ANALYST'S REPORT RE: ASSEMBLY BILL NO.

2854 (Dunlap) (Aug. 20, 1974). The one truly significant open space easement created under the 1969 Act is in Los Angeles County. A fifty-year grant, it protects 40,000 acres on the unique Santa Catalina Island. *See* discussion in Santa Catalina Island Conservancy v. County of Los Angeles, 126 Cal. App. 3d 221 (1981).

33. Enrolled Bill Report of the State Resources Agency re: AB 2854 (Dunlap) (Sept. 13, 1974).

34. AB 2854 (Dunlap), Stats. 1974, ch. 1003, § 2, at 2154, Cal. Gov't Code §§ 51070–51097.

35. Legislative Analyst's Report, *supra* note 32.

36. Telephone interview with Leonard Goldberg, administrative assistant to Assemblyman Thomas Bates (author of the Conservation Easements Act of 1979) (Oct. 1, 1979).

37. Enrolled Bill Report of the State Office of Planning and Research re: SB 1209 (Dunlap) (Sept. 12, 1977). *See also* State of Cal., Office of Plan. & Research, Saving the Good Earth: What California Counties Are Doing to Conserve Agricultural Land 11 (1981).

38. *See* letter of State Senator John F. Dunlap (author, SB 1029) to Governor Edmund G. Brown, Jr. (May 10, 1977).

39. SB 1029 (Dunlap), Stats. 1977, ch. 1178, §§ 1–15, at 3859.

40. *See* letter of Joseph Janelli, California Farm Bureau Federation, to Willie Brown, chairman, Assembly Committee on Revenue and Taxation (Aug. 5, 1977).

41. AB 245 (Bates), Stats. 1979, ch. 179, § 1, at 398, Cal Civ. Code §§ 815–816.

42. *See* p. 56.

43. Cal. Rev. & Tax. Code §§ 17299.1, 18052.2, 24441, 24916.2.

44. *See In re* Los Angeles County Pioneer Society, 40 Cal. 2d 852 (1953), *cert. denied* 346 U.S. 888, *reh'g denied*, 346 U.S. 928 (1953).

45. Cal. Rev. & Tax. Code §§ 421–423. *See* pp. 73–75.

46. The relationship of the Open-Space Easement Act to the federal legislation is discussed in Chapter Two.

47. Cal. Gov't Code § 16140.

48. *See* Senate Comm. on Natural Resources & Wildlife, Analysis of AB 245 (June 13, 1979).

49. For a review of the law governing common law easements, restrictive covenants and equitable servitudes, *see* p. 113 and following.

50. Amended by AB 470 (Bates), Stats. 1981, ch. 478, § 1, at __.

51. *See* UNITED STATES DEP'T OF THE INTERIOR, ASSISTANT SEC-RETARY FOR FISH & WILDLIFE & PARKS, PROPOSED LAND PROTEC-TION POLICY FOR THE LAND AND WATER CONSERVATION FUND (Draft) (July 12, 1981). *See also* Policy for the Use of the Federal Portion of the Land and Water Conservation Fund, 47 Fed. Reg. 19,784 (1982).

52. The before-and-after donation valuation is the federal standard for determining the deductible amount a donation will yield. *See* p. 59. For a more detailed discussion of the effect of a conservation easement on property taxes, *see* pp. 75–77.

53. *See* AB 3657 (Bates) (Apr. 4, 1978).

54. *See* MILLER & STARR, CURRENT LAW OF CALIFORNIA REAL ESTATE § 25:11 (rev. ed. 1977).

55. 3 WITKIN, SUMMARY OF CALIFORNIA LAW 2068 (8th ed. 1973).

56. *See* 3 R. POWELL, THE LAW OF REAL PROPERTY § 422 (1979).

57. Whyte, *supra* note 17, at 55.

58. PRELIMINARY REPORT, *supra* note 13, at 29.

59. *Id.* at 23.

60. *See* REVIEW OF THE CALIFORNIA LAND CONSERVATION ACT, *supra* note 27, at 7–11.

61. *See* p. 73.

62. CONSTITUTIONAL TASK FORCE ON ARTICLE XIII, PROPOSED REVISION OF ARTICLE XIII, CALIFORNIA CONSTITUTION 18 (May 6, 1974).

63. *See* AB 2770 (Sher), 1982 Stats., ch. 1489, § 2, at __. In addition to renaming the Act, AB 2770 added the important policy statements contained in §§ 51101–51103.

64. CAL. REV. & TAX. CODE §§ 431–437. *See* p. 75. The constitutional authority for this special system of timberland taxation is contained in CAL. CONST. art. XIII, § 3(j).

65. The Legislative Counsel's Digest to AB 597 (Sher), Stats. 1982, ch. 711, at __ (amending the Regional Park and Open-Space Districts Law) creates the impression that subventions will be available when regional park and open space districts accept open space easements. AB 597 makes no provision for this, however, and CAL. GOV'T CODE § 16141 would seem to preclude it.

66. Although the term "open-space easement" is used in the 1982 amendment, there is no apparent link between this legislation and the Open-Space Easement Act. Park or open space districts are

qualified to hold easements under Section 815.3(b) of the Conservation Easements Act.

67. Senate Legislative Committee Comment, CAL. GOV'T CODE § 831.2, WEST'S ANNOTATED CALIFORNIA CODES.

68. *See, e.g.,* Darr v. Lone Starr Indus., 94 Cal. App. 3d 895 (1979) (specific holding that owner of right-of-way easement not protected by § 846 superseded by subsequent amendment of § 846). *See also* Baldwin v. State of Cal., 6 Cal. 3d 424, 435 (1972) (liability is the rule, immunity the exception).

69. CAL. CODE OF CIV. PROC. § 1240.610.

70. CAL. CODE OF CIV. PROC. § 1235.170.

71. *See* CAL. CODE OF CIV. PROC. §§ 1240.030 and 1245.250. Section 1240.030 sets forth the three issues of public necessity that are normally concluded by a public entity's resolution under § 1245.250: (a) the public interest and necessity require the project; (b) the project is planned or located in the manner that will be most compatible with the greatest public good and the least private injury; and (c) the property sought to be acquired is necessary for the project.

72. CAL. PUB. RES. CODE §§ 30000–30900.

73. CAL. PUB. RES. CODE § 30001.5.

74. 1964–2 C.B. 62.

75. I.R.S. News Release No. 784 (Nov. 15, 1965), 657 CCH 6787.

76. Pub. L. No. 91-172, 83 Stat. 487.

77. I.R.C. § 170(f)(3)(B)(ii).

78. H.R. REP. No. 782, 91st Cong., 1st Sess. 294 (1969).

79. Treas. Reg. 1.170A-7(b)(1)(ii).

80. Rev. Rul. 74-583, 1974-2 C.B. 80.

81. Rev. Rul. 75-358, 1975-2 C.B. 76.

82. Rev. Rul. 75-373, 1975-2 C.B. 77.

83. Small, *The Tax Benefits of Donating Easements in Scenic and Historic Property*, 7 REAL EST. L.J. 304, 310 (1979); *see also* Browne & Van Dorn, *Charitable Gifts of Partial Interests in Real Property for Conservation Purposes*, 29 TAX LAW. 67, 75 (1975).

84. Pub. L. No. 94-455, 90 Stat. 1520.

85. Pub. L. No. 95-30, 91 Stat. 126.

86. The 1976 Act allowed easements for a minimum thirty-year term. The 1977 Act amended to permit only easements in perpetuity. Perpetual easements are undoubtedly more effective land conservation tools. Historic preservationists, however, are said to

favor a term easement deduction. *See* Small, *supra* note 83, at 315–318.

87. *See* IRS Private Letter Rulings No. 7734023 (May 24, 1977) and No. 8012026 (Dec. 27, 1979); *see also* IRS, National Office Technical Advice Memorandum, Index No. 0170.16–02 (Apr. 14, 1980).

88. *See* H.R. REP. No. 263, 95th Cong., 1st Sess. 30 (1977).

89. Pub. L. No. 96-541, § 6, 94 Stat. 3204.

90. *See* H.R. REP. No. 1278, 96th Cong., 2d Sess. 18 (1980); S. REP. No. 1007, 96th Cong., 2d Sess. 13 (1980). There are only minor differences in language between these two reports. The Senate Report is cited throughout this chapter because it is slightly more expansive than the House Report.

91. Official notice, published on October 28, 1982, stated that the proposed regulations were in the office of the Commissioner of the Internal Revenue Service where they had been since April 14, 1982, awaiting formal approval. *See* 47 Fed. Reg. 48,701 (1982). In a January 3, 1983, telephone interview with John Harman of the Chief Counsel's Office at IRS, the author was informed that the regulations were still under "policy review," and that it was impossible to predict when they would be released. The delay in issuing regulations has had a chilling effect on many conservation easement programs. *See, e.g.,* letter from Senator John Warner to Secretary of the Treasury Donald Regan (May 7, 1982). Congressional action to bypass the IRS regulations and to increase the tax incentives for donating conservation easements is now a possibility. *See* S. 3024, 97th Cong., 2d Sess., 128 CONG. REC. 13333-13336 (introduced by Senator Wallop of Wyoming on Oct. 1, 1982). Pressure to create "safe harbor" categories for easement donations—such as easements granted to or approved by governmental entities—is also developing. *See Id.* and H.R. 7226 (Byron), 97th Cong., 2d Sess. (1982).

92. *See* H.R. REP. No. 1278 and S. REP. No. 1007, *supra* note 90.

93. *See* S. REP. No. 1007, *supra* note 90, at 10.

94. *Id.* at 14.

95. *Id.*

96. *Id.*

97. There are reports that Treasury could complicate matters by narrowly interpreting the qualified real property interest requirement to exclude conservation easements that permit the donor to retain any mineral rights. *See* Michael Dennis, Conservation Ease-

ment Regulations (Dec. 17, 1981) (unpublished memorandum of The Nature Conservancy).

98. *See Miscellaneous Tax Bills: Charitable Deduction for Certain Contributions of Real Property for Conservation Purposes: Hearings on H.R. 4611 before the Subcomm. on Select Revenue Measures of the House Comm. on Ways and Means,* 96th Cong., 1st Sess. (1979) at 6 and 12 (statement of Daniel I. Halperin, deputy assistant secretary of the U.S. Treasury Dep't).

99. *Id.*

100. *See Minor Tax Bills: Deductions for Contributions of Certain Interests in Property for Conservation Purposes: Hearings on H.R. 7318 before the Subcomm. on Select Revenue Measures of the House Comm. on Ways and Means,* 96th Cong., 2d Sess. (1980) at 165–168 (statement of Daniel I. Halperin, deputy assistant secretary of the U.S. Treasury Dep't).

101. S. REP. No. 1007, *supra* note 90, at 10.

102. *See Id.*

103. *Id.* at 13.

104. *See Id.*

105. *Id.* at 12.

106. *Id.* at 10–11.

107. *Id.* at 11.

108. *Id.*

109. *See Id.*

110. *Id.*

111. *Id.*

112. *See Id.*

113. *Id.*

114. *See Id.*

115. *See Id.* at 10.

116. *Id.* at 12.

117. *Id.*

118. *Id.*

119. *Id.*

120. *See Hearings on H.R. 7318, supra* note 100, at 167 (statement of Daniel I. Halperin, deputy assistant secretary of the U.S. Treasury Dep't).

121. *See* S. REP. No. 1007, *supra* note 90, at 15.

122. *See* Rev. Rul. 73-339, 1973-2 C.B. 68; *see also* Thayer v. Commissioner, 36 T.C.M. (CCH) 1504 (1977).

123. *See* Rev. Rul. 79-24, 1979-1 C.B. 565.

124. S. Rep. No. 1007, *supra* note 90, at 15.

125. *Id.*

126. *Id.*

127. *Id; see also* Rev. Rul. 76-376, 1976-2 C.B. 53.

128. *Id.; see also* Thayer v. Commissioner, 36 T.C.M. (CCH) 1504 (1977).

129. *See* Rev. Rul. 64-205, 1964-2 C.B. 62.

130. *Id.*

131. *See* Rev. Rul. 67-461, 1967-2 C.B. 125.

132. Treas. Reg. 1.170A-a(e).

133. S. Rep. No. 1007, *supra* note 90, at 13.

134. *Id.* at 14.

135. *Id.*

136. Arthur B. Daugherty, Open Space Preservation: Federal Tax Policies Encouraging Donation of Conservation Easements, U.S. Dep't of Agriculture 5, ESCS-32 (1978).

137. *See Hearings on H.R. 4611, supra* note 98, at 12 (statement of Daniel I. Halperin, deputy assistant secretary of the Treasury); *see also* Note, *The California Open-Space Easement Act: The Efficacy of Indirect Incentives,* 16 Santa Clara L. Rev. 359, 367 (1976).

138. *See* Rev. Rul. 73-339, 1973-2 C.B. 68, 69.

139. *See* Scheffres v. Commissioner, 28 T.C.M. (CCH) 234 (1969); *see also* Seldin v. Commissioner, 28 T.C.M. (CCH) 1215 (1969) (contribution by developers of land for school enhanced value of development but was freely made).

140. *See* Stubbs v. United States, 428 F.2d 885 (9th Cir. 1970), *cert. denied,* 400 U.S. 1009 (1971) (dedication of land conditioned on favorable zoning). *See also* Karl D. Petit v. Commissioner, 61 T.C. 634 (1974) (land dedicated to city in exchange for subdivision approval); Jordon Perlmutter v. Commissioner, 45 T.C. 311 (1965) (land dedicated to county in order to comply with subdivision ordinance).

141. The one case where the economic benefit received did not flow directly and immediately out of a bargained for exchange, Larry G. Sutton v. Commissioner, 57 T.C. 239 (1971) (grantor took initial steps to develop property ten months after conveyance that resulted in rezoning), was disapproved by the Ninth Circuit Court of Appeals .in Colman v. Commissioner, 511 F.2d 1263 (1975). For a survey of the cases, *see* Annot., 30 A.L.R. Fed. 796 (1976).

142. Treas. Reg. 1-170A-1(e).

143. *See* Sierra Club v. City of Hayward, 28 Cal. 3d 849 (1981) (narrowly construing the acceptable grounds for cancellation). The Williamson Act was amended following the decision in Sierra Club v. City of Hayward to specify in detail the circumstances justifying cancellation. *See* AB 2074 (Robinson), Stats. 1981, ch. 1095, § 1, at __. The court's interpretation was not rejected, but the standards for cancellation were relaxed somewhat from those the court imposed. Nevertheless, Sierra Club v. City of Hayward remains instructive. Taking a statewide view of the public's interest in open space, the court has shown that it will strictly enforce the land conservation legislation against local attempts to weaken it.

144. Treas. Reg. 1.170A-1(e).

145. *See* Kingsbury Browne, Conservation Easements: I.R.S. Private Ruling: Use of Revocable Trust and *In Terrorem* Clause (Nov. 7, 1977) (unpublished memorandum).

146. J. MERTENS, LAW OF FEDERAL TAXATION § 7.34 (rev. ed. 1969); *see also* Alice Phelan Sullivan Corp. v. United States, 381 F.2d 399 (1967); Rev. Rul. 76-150, 1976-1 C.B. 38.

147. *See Hearings on H.R. 7318, supra* note 100, at 223.

148. Letter from Senator Malcolm Wallop (Wyoming) to Donald Regan, secretary of the U.S. Treasury Dep't (Nov. 19, 1981).

149. S. REP. NO. 1007, *supra* note 90 at 13.

150. *See* PROPOSED LAND PROTECTION POLICY FOR THE LAND AND WATER CONSERVATION FUND and Policy for Use of the Federal Portion of the Land and Water Conservation Fund, *supra* note 51.

151. *See* PROPOSED LAND PROTECTION POLICY, *supra* note 51, at 15.

152. 16 U.S.C. § 1285.

153. DAUGHERTY, *supra* note 136, at 24.

154. Pub. L. No. 97-34, 95 Stat. 1972.

155. *Cong. Index* 2 (ICH) No. 29, Aug. 6, 1981.

156. *See* Harl, *Special Use Valuation: an Exercise in Fence Building,* 68 A.B.A.J. 50 (Jan. 1982).

157. Browne & Van Dorn, *supra* note 83, at 72.

158. *See* Treas. Reg. 1.170A-4(c)(1)(ii).

159. AB 1827 (Naylor), Stats. 1982, ch. 195, §§ 10, 11, 29, 30 at __; AB 2595 (Deddeh), Stats. 1982, ch. 1558, §§ 8 and 39.5, at __.

160. CAL. REV. & TAX. CODE § 14104.5 (added by AB 369 (Deddeh), Stats 1982, ch. 220, § 4, at __.

161. The informal opinion of Myron Siedorf, chief inheritance

tax attorney of the State Controller's Office, conveyed to the author by John Shell of the Controller's Office (in response to a telephone inquiry on Nov. 18, 1982), is that CAL. GOV'T CODE §§ 7301–7309 are no longer operative in light of the Inheritance Tax repeal.

162. *See* REVIEW OF THE CALIFORNIA LAND CONSERVATION ACT, *supra* note 27, at 15.

163. See AB 3657 (Bates) (Apr. 4, 1978).

164. Telephone interview with Leonard Goldberg, administrative assistant to Assemblyman Tom Bates (author of Section 815) (Oct. 1, 1979).

165. ASSEMBLY COMM. ON RESOURCES, LAND USE & ENERGY, ANALYSIS OF AB 245 (Willoughby); *see also* SENATE COMM. ON NATURAL RESOURCES & WILDLIFE, ANALYSIS OF AB 245 (June 13, 1979).

166. REVIEW OF THE CALIFORNIA LAND CONSERVATION ACT, *supra* note 27.

167. *Id.* at 15.

168. *See Id.* at 18.

169. AB 971 (Bergeson), Stats. 1982, ch. 67, § 20, at 67; AB 2308 (Bates), Stats. 1982, ch. 1485, § 1, at __. The Section was tightened somewhat to prevent a perceived misuse of the tax exemption laws by large nonexempt landholders, and also was made inapplicable to property that is reserved for future development.

170. 126 Cal. App. 3d 221 (1981). Despite the favorable ruling in this case, the tightening referred to in note 169 has effectively revoked the Santa Catalina Island Conservancy's Section 214.02 exemption.

171. 126 Cal. App. 3d at 237.

172. *See* ASSESSMENT STANDARDS DIV., PROPERTY TAX DEP'T, CAL. STATE BD. OF EQUALIZATION, ASSESSOR'S HANDBOOK, AH 501 (1974); *see also* EHRMAN & FLAVIN, TAXING CALIFORNIA PROPERTY §§ 3.6, 17.9 (2d ed. 1979).

173. *See* CAL. CIV. CODE § 815.1.

174. CAL. CIV. CODE § 1046.

175. *See* Comment, *Real Property: Estates on Condition Subsequent—Extension of the Judicial Bias Against Forfeiture*, 7 HASTINGS L.J. 101 (1955).

176. WITKIN, *supra* note 55, at 1923.

177. *See* CALIFORNIA LAW REVISION COMM'N, RECOMMENDA-

TION RELATING TO MARKETABLE TITLE OF REAL PROPERTY 415–416 (Nov. 1981).

178. *Id.* at 415; *see* CAL. CODE OF CIV. PROC. §§ 319–320.

179. *See* CAL. LAW REVISION COMM'N, *supra* note 177, at 416.

180. *See Id., passim.*

181. *Id.* at 416–417.

182. AB 2416 (McAlister), 1982 Stats., ch. 1268, § 1, at __ , CAL. CIV. CODE § 885.020.

183. CAL. CIV. CODE §§ 885.030 and 885.060. A five-year grace period is provided for existing interests that would otherwise expire sooner by operation of the new law.

184. CAL. CIV. CODE § 885.050.

185. CALIFORNIA LAW REVISION COMM'N, *supra* note 177, at 421.

186. CAL. CIV. CODE § 880.240(c) and (d).

187. *See* CAL. CIV. CODE §§ 715–716.

188. CAL. CIV. CODE § 715.

189. *See* CAL. CIV. CODE §§ 767, 769, 773 and 778. Curiously, AB 2416, *supra* note 182, does not deal with executory interests. However, the Law Revision Commission considers its work in the area unfinished, and a future recommendation is likely to reach such interests. *See* CALIFORNIA LAW REVISION COMM'N, *supra* note 177, at 408.

190. CAL. CIV. CODE § 1442.

191. Hawley v. Kafitz, 148 Cal. 393, 394 (1905).

192. *See* WITKIN, *supra* note 55, at 1924–1927; *see also* MILLER & STARR, *supra* note 54, at § 25:23–25; 2 BOWMAN, OGDEN'S REVISED CALIFORNIA REAL PROPERTY LAW, §§ 23.29–23.34 (1975). The applicability of the doctrine of changed conditions to condition subsequent deeds was codified by AB 2416, § 885.040. An exception is made for obsolescence occurring within the lifetime of the grantor of a conditional fee donated to a tax-exempt organization. For a brief discussion of the doctrine of changed conditions, *see* pp. 117–118.

193. Rosencranz v. Pacific Elec. Ry., 21 Cal. 2d 602, 605 (1943). The recent changes in the law affected by AB 2416 are not intended to relax this tradition of strict construction. *See* CALIFORNIA LAW REVISION COMM'N, *supra* note 177, at 418–419.

194. The term is used by Russell Brenneman in R. BRENNEMAN, PRIVATE APPROACHES TO THE PRESERVATION OF OPEN LAND, THE CONSERVATION AND RESEARCH FOUNDATION (1967).

195. *See* J.T. Fargason, 21 B.T.A. 1032 (1930).

196. Treas. Reg. § 1.170A-1(e); Rev. Rul. 77–148, 1977-1 C.B. 63.

197. Treas. Reg. § 1.170A-7(a) (3).

198. *See* J.T. Fargason, 21 B.T.A. 1032 (1930).

199. Described on pp. 103–104.

200. *See* Thomas, *Transfers of Land to the State for Conservation Purposes: Methods, Guarantees, and Tax Analysis for Prospective Donors*, 36 Ohio St. L.J. 545, 561 (1975).

201. Cal. Gov't Code § 6953.

202. *See* Cal. Pub. Res. Code § 31150.

203. *See* Treas. Reg. § 1.1011-2.

204. *See* Treas. Reg. §§ 1.170A-4(c) (2) and 1.1011-2. It should be noted that a deduction for a bargain sale of ordinary income property, such as land held as inventory by a developer, is available only for the amount by which the bargain price is below the taxpayer's basis in the property. The allocation of basis described in the text is not made and none of the appreciation is deductible. Treas. Reg. § 1.170A-4(a).

205. *See* Kingsbury Browne, Tax Free Land Swaps as a Means of Acquiring Open Space (Apr. 3, 1978) (unpublished memorandum).

206. *See* I.R.C. § 453(B)(f)(1) (added Oct. 19, 1981).

207. *See* Thomas, *supra* note 200, at 561.

208. I.R.C. §§ 170(b)(1)(C) and 170(d).

209. *See* Treas. Reg. § 1.170A-7(b)(1)(i); Rev. Rul. 75-420, 1975-2 C.B. 78.

210. *See* I.R.C. §§ 170(b) and (d).

211. I.R.C. § 170(f)(3)(B)(ii).

212. *See* I.R.C. § 170(f)(3)(B)(i).

213. *See* I.R.C. § 170(f)(4); Treas. Reg. 1-170A-12.

214. *Id.*

215. S. Rep. No. 1007, *supra* note 90, at 10.

216. *See* discussion on p. 99.

217. Under Cal. Civ. Code § 711, provisions that unreasonably restrict a person's power or ability to sell his property are void. *See* Wellenkamp v. Bank of Am., 21 Cal. 3d 943 (1978). The reasonableness of a given restriction is determined by weighing the "quantum of restraint" against the justification advanced for it. *See Id.* at 949.

218. "In the absence of statute, there is no limitation upon the duration of an estate for years," Brenneman, *supra* note 194, at 33. Although a perpetual lease would approximate the transfer of a fee,

the lessor would retain a reversion empowering him or his assignee to enforce the terms of the lease. *See also* Fisher v. Parsons, 213 Cal. App. 2d 829 (1963), and the following annotations: 3 A.L.R. 498 (1919), 162 A.L.R. 1147 (1946), 31 A.L.R. 2d 607 (1953).

219. *See* Fisher v. Parsons, 213 Cal. App. 2d 829 (1963). *See also* 3 A.L.R. 498 (1919), 162 A.L.R. 1147 (1946), 31 A.L.R. 2d 607 (1953).

220. CAL. CIV. CODE § 715.

221. *See* BRENNEMAN, *supra* note 194, at 33–34.

222. Uniform Supervision of Trustees for Charitable Purposes Act, CAL. GOV'T CODE §§ 12580–12597.

223. CAL. GOV'T CODE § 12588.

224. CAL. GOV'T CODE § 12591.

225. BRENNEMAN, *supra* note 194, at 19.

226. *See* I.R.C. § 170(f)(2); Treas. Reg. 1.170A-6(a)(1).

227. BOWMAN, *supra* note 192, at 537.

228. CAL. CIV. CODE §§ 802, 1044; 3 WITKIN, *supra* note 55, at 2068.

229. *See* BOWMAN, *supra* note 192, at 546–547 (1974); Jersey Farm Co. v. Atlanta Realty Co., 164 Cal. 412 (1912).

230. *Id.* at 551.

231. WITKIN, *supra* note 55, at 2068–2074.

232. *Id.* at 2070.

233. POWELL, *supra* note 56.

234. *See* discussion on p. 99.

235. CAL. CIV. CODE § 1468.

236. *See* Note, *Covenants and Equitable Servitudes in California*, 29 HASTINGS L.J. 545, 546 (1978).

237. *See Id.* at 551.

238. *Id.* at 566.

239. *See* Werner v. Graham, 181 Cal. 174 (1919); Thrams v. Starrett, 34 Cal. App. 3d 766 (1973).

240. *Id.*

241. *See* Note, *supra* note 236, at 571.

242. *Id.* at 572.

243. *See* MILLER & STARR, *supra* note 54.

244. S. REP. NO. 1007, *supra* note 90, at 10.

SELECTED BIBLIOGRAPHY

Alden, R. F., and M. J. Shockro. "Preferential Assessment of Agricultural Lands: Preservation or Discrimination." 42 *S. Cal. L. Rev.* 54 (1969).

Association of Bay Area Governments. *Regional Open Space Plan Phase II, San Francisco Bay Region.* 1972.

Beckwith, James, Jr. "Developments in the Law of Historic Preservation and a Reflection on Liberty." 12 *Wake Forest L. Rev.* 93 (1976).

Boasberg, Tersh. "Federal Tax Problems Arising from Real Estate Activities of Non-Profit Preservation Organizations." 8 *Urb. L. Rev.* 1 (1976).

Booth, Richard. "Developing Institutions for Regional Land Use Planning and Control—The Adirondack Experience." 28 *Buffalo L. Rev.* 645 (1979).

Bowden, Gerald. "Article XVIII—Opening the Door to Open Space Control." 1 *Pac. L.J.* 461 (1970).

Bowman, Arthur. *Ogden's Revised California Real Property Law.* Berkeley: California Continuing Education of the Bar. 1974.

Brenneman, Russell. *Private Approaches to the Preservation of Open Land.* The Conservation and Research Foundation. 1967.

Browne, Kingsbury, and Walter Van Dorn. "Charitable Gifts of Partial Interests in Real Property for Conservation Purposes." 29 *Tax Law.* 67 (1975).

California Legislature. Joint Committee on Open Space Lands. *Final Report.* 1970.

California Legislature. Joint Committee on Open Space Lands. *Preliminary Report.* March 1969.

California Legislature. Joint Committee on Open Space Lands. Citizens Technical Advisory Committee. *Semi-Final Report.* August 1969.

California Legislature. Joint Committee on Open Space Lands. *State Open Space and Resource Conservation Program for California.* 1972.

California Legislature. Joint Committee on Open Space Lands.

Techniques and General Legal Aspects of Preserving Open Space. October 1971.

Charmichael, Donald. "Transferable Development Rights as a Basis for Land Use Control." 2 *Fla. St. U.L. Rev.* 35 (1974).

Chavooshian, Budd, and Thomas Norman. "Transfer of Development Rights: A New Concept in Land-Use Management." Appraisal J., July 1975, at 400.

Comment. "Assessment of Farmland under California Land Conservation Act and Breathing Space Amendment." 55 *Calif. L. Rev.* 273 (1967).

Comment. "Conservation Restrictions: A Survey." 8 *Conn. L. Rev.* 383 (1976).

Comment. "Dilemma of Preserving Open Space Land—How to Make Californians an Offer They Can't Refuse." 13 *Santa Clara Law.* 284 (1973).

Comment. "Preserving Rural Land Resources: The California Westside." 1 *Ecology L.Q.* 330 (1971).

Comment. "Real Property: Estates on Condition Subsequent—Extension of the Judicial Bias Against Forfeiture." 7 *Hastings L.J.* 101 (1955).

Comment. "Techniques for Preserving Open Spaces." 75 *Harv. L. Rev.* 1622 (1962).

Committee Report. "State and Local Property Taxation in Light of Proposition XIII and Similar Taxing Measures." 15 *Real Prop., Prob. & Tr. J.* 501 (1980).

Conservation Law Foundation of New England. *Conservation Restrictions.* March 1976.

Costonis, John. "Development Rights Transfer: Easing the Police Power—Eminent Domain Deadlock." 26 *Land Use Law & Zoning Dig.* 6 (1974).

Currier, Barry. "An Analysis of Differential Taxation as a Method of Maintaining Agricultural and Open Space Land Uses." 11 *Land Use & Envtl. L. Rev.* 443 (1980).

Daugherty, Arthur. *Open Space Preservation: Federal Tax Policies Encouraging Donation of Conservation Easements.* United States Department of Agriculture, Economics, Statistics and Cooperatives Service. ESCS-32. 1978.

Davis, Arthur. *State Land Use Programs: Reality or Illusion?* Lincoln Institute of Land Policy. Land Policy Roundtable Policy Analysis, Series No. 203. 1979.

Day, Christian. "Federal Income Tax Reform: An Important Tool for Historic Preservation." 16 *Wake Forest L. Rev.* 315 (1980).

Dean, John. "The California Conservation Act of 1965 and the Fight to Save California's Prime Agricultural Lands." 30 *Hastings L.J.* 1859 (1979).

Department of Housing and Urban Development. *Open Space for Urban America.* 1965.

Dunham, Allison. *Preservation of Open Areas: A Study of the Non-Governmental Role.* Welfare Council of Metropolitan Chicago. 1966.

Eckert, Robert J. "Acquisition of Development Rights: A Modern Land Use Tool." 23 *U. Miami L. Rev.* 347 (1969).

Ehrman, Kenneth, and Sean Flavin. *Taxing California Real Property.* 2d ed. Palo Alto: Bull Publishing Co., 1979.

Endangered Harvest: The Future of Bay Area Farmland. Report of the Farmlands Conservation Project of People for Open Space. 1980.

Englebrecht, Ted, and Robert Jamison. "An Empirical Inquiry into the Role of the Tax Court in the Valuation of Property for Charitable Contribution Purposes." LIV *Acct. Rev.* 554 (1979).

Federal Tax Benefits and Land Conservation. Edited by K. Browne. 1979. Transcript of meeting sponsored by the Brandywine Conservancy at Chadds Ford, Pennsylvania, September 29, 1979.

Fenner, Randee Gorin. "Land Trusts: An Alternative Method of Preserving Open Space." 33 *Vand. L. Rev.* 1039 (1980).

Gunning, Harold. "Valuation of Restrictive Easements." 31 *Appraisal J.* 29 (1963).

Hembrick, Kenton. "Charitable Donations of Conservation Easements: Valuation, Enforcement and Public Benefit." 59 *Taxes* (CCH) 347 (1981).

Herring, Francis, ed. *Open Space and the Law.* Institute of Governmental Studies. Berkeley: University of California, 1965.

Hillis, Phillips, Cairncross, Clark & Martin. *San Juan County: Private Preservation Techniques.* February 24, 1977.

Hoose, Phillip M. *Building an Ark: Tools for the Preservation of Natural Diversity through Land Protection.* Covelo, Ca.: Island Press, 1981.

Jordahl, Richard. "Conservation and Scenic Easements: An Experience Resume." 39 *Land Econ.* 343 (1963).

Kent, T.J. *Open Space for the San Francisco Bay Area: Orga-*

nizing to Guide Metropolitan Growth. Institute of Governmental Studies. Berkeley: University of California, 1970.

Kinnamon, David. "Tax Incentives for Sensible Land Use Through Gifts of Conservation Easements." 15 *Real Prop.. Prob. & Tr. J.* 1 (1980).

Kliman, Burton. "The Use of Conservation Restrictions on Historic Properties as Charitable Donations for Federal Income Tax Purposes." 9 *B.C. Envtl. Aff. L. Rev.* 513 (1981).

Knight, Robert, and Nancy Dye. "Attorney's Guide to Montana Conservation Easements." 42 *Mont. L. Rev.* 21 (1981).

Krasnowiecki, Jan, and James Paul. "The Preservation of Open Space in Metropolitan Areas." 110 *U. Pa. L. Rev.* 179 (1961).

Kratovil, Robert. "Divided Interests in Land: Enforcement Problems Under Modern Concepts of Property Law." 14 *Hous. L. Rev.* 583 (1977).

Land, Alan. "Unraveling the Rurban Fringe: Proposal for Implementing Proposition 3." 19 *Hastings L.J.* 421 (1968).

Maryland Environmental Trust. *Conservation Easements.* Rev. ed. June 1977.

Menikoff, Jerry. "The Taxation of Restricted Use Property: A Theoretical Framework." 27 *Buffalo L. Rev.* 419 (1978).

Miller, Harry, and Marvin Starr. *Current Law of California Real Estate.* San Francisco: Bancroft-Whitney, 1975.

Milne, Janet. *The Landowner's Options: A Guide to the Voluntary Protection of Land in Maine.* The Maine Critical Areas Program. State Planning Office and Maine Coast Heritage Trust, June 1977.

Minor Tax Bills: Deductions for Contributions of Certain Interests in Property for Conservation Purposes: Hearings on H.R. 7318 before the Subcommittee on Select Revenue Measures of the House Committee on Ways and Means, 96th Cong., 2d Sess., 1980.

Miscellaneous Revenue Act of 1980. Report of the Committee on Ways and Means, U.S. House of Representatives, together with additional views on H.R. 7956. H.R. Rep. No. 1278, 96th Cong., 2d Sess., 1980.

Miscellaneous Tax Bills: Charitable Deduction for Certain Contributions of Real Property for Conservation Purposes: Hearings on H.R. 4611 before the Subcommittee on Select Revenue Measures of the House Committee on Ways and Means, 96th Cong., 1st Sess., 1979.

Mix, Averill. "Restricted Use Assessment in California: Can it Fulfill its Objectives?" 11 *Santa Clara Law.* 259 (1971).

Montana Land Reliance and the Land Trust Exchange. *Private Options: Tools and Concepts for Land Conservation.* Covelo, Ca.: Island Press, 1982.

Moore, Marvin. "The Acquisition and Preservation of Open Lands." 23 *Wash. & Lee L. Rev.* 274 (1966).

Nelson, Bryan E. "Differential Assessment of Agricultural Land in Kansas: A Discussion and Proposal." 25 *Kan. L. Rev.* 215 (1977).

Netherton, Ross. "Environmental Conservation and Historic Preservation through Recorded Land Use Agreements." 14 *Real Prop., Prob. & Tr. J.* 540 (1979).

Note. "Appraisal of Techniques to Preserve Open Space." 9 *Vill. L. Rev.* 559 (1964).

Note. "Coastal Land Preservation: Obstacles to Effective State Action." 4 *Colum J. Envtl. L.* 254 (1978).

Note. "Conservation and Preservation Restriction Seminar." 16 *N.H. B.J.,* June 1975, at 310.

Note. "Covenants and Equitable Servitudes in California." 29 *Hastings L.J.* 545 (1978).

Note. "Easements to Preserve Open Space Land." 1 *Ecology L.Q.* 728 (1971).

Note. "Preservation of Indiana's Scenic Areas: A Method." 40 *Ind. L.J.* 402 (1965).

Note. "Preservation of Open Space through Scenic Easements and Greenbelt Zoning." 12 *Stan. L. Rev.* 638 (1960).

Note. "Scenic Easements." 8 *Idaho L. Rev.* 131 (1971).

Note. "The California Open-Space Easement Act: The Efficacy of Indirect Incentives." 16 *Santa Clara L. Rev.* 359 (1976).

Plimpton, Oakes. *Conservation Easements: Legal Analysis of "Conservation Easements" as a Method of Privately Conserving and Preserving Land.* 1966. Unpublished memorandum prepared for The Nature Conservancy.

Powell. R. *The Law of Real Property.* New York: Matthew Bender, 1979.

Reynolds, Judith. "Preservation Easements." *Appraisal J.,* July 1976, at 355.

Roe, Charles. "Innovative Techniques to Preserve Rural Land

Resources." 5 *Envtl. Aff.* 419 (1976).

Rose, Jerome. "Psychological, Legal and Administrative Problems of the Proposal to Use the Transfer of Development Rights as a Technique to Preserve Open Space." 51 *J. Urb. L.* 471 (1974).

Schroeder, William. "Preservation and Control of Open Space in Metropolitan Areas." 5 *Ind. Legal F.* 345 (1971).

Sicard, Russell R. "Pursuing Open Space Preservation: The Massachusetts Conservation Restriction." 4 *Envtl. Aff.* 481 (1975).

Silverstone, Samuel. "Open Space Preservation Through Conservation Easements." 12 *Osgoode Hall L.J.* (1974).

Simes, Lewis. "Restricting Land Use in California by Rights of Entry and Possibilities of Reverter." 13 *Hastings L.J.* 293 (1962).

Small, Stephen. "The Tax Benefits of Donating Easements in Scenic and Historic Property." 7 *Real Est. L.J.* 304 (1979).

State of California. California Law Revision Commission. *Recommendation Relating to Marketable Title of Real Property.* November 1981.

State of California. Department of Finance. *A Review of the California Land Conservation Act.* Report No. 580-8. October 1980.

Sussna, Stephen. "New Tools for Open Space Preservation." 2 *Urb. L.* 87 (1970).

Sutte, Donald, and Roger Cunningham. *Scenic Easements: Legal, Administrative and Valuation Problems and Procedures.* Highway Research Board of the National Academy of Sciences—National Research Council. National Cooperative Highway Research Program Report No. 56. 1968.

Symposium of Land Use Planning. 19 *Nat. Resources J.* 1 (1979).

Tax Treatment Extension Act of 1980. Report of the Committee on Finance. U.S. Senate on H.R. 6975. S. Rep. No. 1007, 96th Cong., 2d Sess., 1980.

The Federal Drive to Acquire Private Lands Should Be Reassessed. Report by the Comptroller General of the U.S. to the Subcommittee on National Parks and Insular Affairs. House Committee on Interior and Insular Affairs, December 14, 1979.

Thomas, Alexander. "Transfers of Land to the State for Conservation Purposes: Methods, Guarantees, and Tax Analysis for Prospective Donors." 36 *Ohio St. L.J.* 545 (1975).

U.S. Department of Commerce. National Oceanic and Atmospheric Administration. Office of Coastal Zone Management. *Shorefront Access and Island Preservation Study.* 1976.

U.S. Department of Commerce. National Oceanic and Atmospheric Administration. Office of Coastal Zone Management. *The Use of Less-than-Fee Simple Acquisition as a Land Management Tool for Coastal Programs, Summary Report.* 1978.

U.S. Department of the Interior. Assistant Secretary for Fish and Wildlife and Parks. *Proposed Land Protection Policy for the Land and Water Conservation Fund.* Draft. July 12, 1981.

U.S. Department of the Interior. *Protecting Nature's Estate.* December 1975.

Volpert, Richard. "Creation and Maintenance of Open Spaces in Subdivisions: Another Approach." 12 *U.C.L.A. L. Rev.* 830 (1965).

Whyte, William. *Securing Open Space for Urban America.* Urban Land Institute Technical Bulletin, No. 36, 1959.

Whyte, William. *The Last Landscape.* Garden City, N.Y.: Doubleday, 1968.

Williams, Howard, and W. D. Davis. "Effect of Scenic Easements on Market Value of Real Property." 36 *Appraisal J.* 15 (1968).

Willis, R. T. "The Use of Easements to Preserve Oregon Open Space." 12 *Willamette L.J.* 124 (1975–1976).

Witkin, Bernard. *Summary of California Law.* 8th ed. San Francisco: Bancroft-Whitney, 1973.

INDEX

Abandonment, easement, 24–26, 27, 33, 60–68 passim, 114
Abandonment fees, 25, 27
Acknowledgment, in easement instrument, 93–94
Affirmative easements, 28, 46, 113
Agricultural lands, 2, 14
  easement instrument covering, 88, 90
  estate tax and, 70
  greenbelt statute and, 10–11
  income tax deduction for, 57, 58
  leased, 110
  Proposition 4 and, 12–13
  Proposition 13 and, 78
  purchase and sell-back arrangement with, 103
  Williamson Act and, 13, 16, 21, 35
Appalachian Trail, 4
Appurtenant easement, 28, 113, 115
Article XIII (California Constitution), 36–37, 73, 74, 76, 77
  and open space easements, 24, 26, 39
  and welfare exemption, 78
Article XIIIA (California Constitution). See Proposition 13
Article XXVIII (California Constitution), 14–15, 36, 73
Assessment valuation. See Valuation
Assignment, easement instrument stating, 92
Atlantic states, 5–6

Bargain sale, 102, 103–104, 154n204
Before-and-after method, 59
Blue Ridge Parkway, 4

California Coastal Act, 43, 55
California Coastal Conservancy. See State Coastal Conservancy

California Constitution. See Article XIII; Article XIIIA; Article XXVIII
California Finance Department, 72–73
California Fish and Game Department, 44
California Land Conservation Act. See Williamson Act
California law codes. See Civil Code; Code of Civil Procedure; Government Code; Public Resources Code; Revenue and Taxation Code
California Law Revision Commission, 98, 153n189
California Park and Recreation Department, 5, 39–40, 44
California Public Works Board, 41, 43
California Resources Agency, 16, 37, 39, 72–73
California state governmental entities (general)
  and defeasible fee grants, 99
  easements held by, 30, 31, 64
  and restrictive covenants/equitable servitudes, 118
California state grants, 39–40
California Supreme Court, 67, 79, 100
California taxes. See under Taxes
California Timberland Productivity Act, 38
California Transportation Department, 42
Cancellation, of Williamson Act contracts, 35, 67, 151n143
Cancellation fees, 35
Capital gains taxes, 71, 102, 103, 104, 105

Changed conditions, doctrine of, 32–34, 117–118, 153n192
Charitable deductions. *See* Income tax deductions
Charitable organizations, 49, 52, 64, 79, 99–100, 112–113. *See also* Nonprofit conservation organizations
Civil Code
  Section 711, 109
  Sections 717–718, 110
  Sections 801–802, 113–114
  Sections 815–816, 27–34, 39, 64, 75–77, 121–123. *See also* Conservation Easements Act
  Section 846, 40, 41
  Section 1217, 116
  Section 1468, 116, 117
Coastal Act, California, 43, 55
Coastal Conservancy. *See* State Coastal Conservancy
Coastal lands, 42–44, 57
Coastal Zone Conservation Act, 43
Code of Civil Procedure, Section 1240, 42
Columbia State Historic Park, 5
Common law, 3, 28–30, 64, 96–101, 115
Common law easement, 32–33, 113–114
Condemnation, 42, 64, 67–68
Conference Committee, 46, 47
Conservation easements, 119
  vs. common law easements, 32–33, 113, 115
  and defeasible fee grants, 96, 99
  defined, 7–8, 29
  drafting of, 81–94
  legislation related to, 9–44, 121–134
  vs. restrictive covenants/equitable servitudes, 28, 32, 115
  sample of, 135–141
  tax incentives for, 9–40 passim, 45–80, 119
Conservation Easements Act, California, 9, 19, 20, 27–34, 39, 120
  and common law easements, 32–33, 114
  and defeasible fee grants, 96, 101
  easement instrument observing, 84, 86
  and income tax deductions, 19–20, 31, 60, 61, 63, 64, 84
  and property tax, 19–20, 31, 75–77
  and restrictive covenants/equitable servitudes, 28, 32, 117, 118
  and subventions, 38
  text of, 121–123
Conservation organizations. *See* Nonprofit conservation organizations
Conservation purposes
  defined, 47, 49–50
  easement instrument specifying, 82, 84–86
Consistency, easement instrument determining, 81–82, 85
Constitution, California. *See* Article XIII; Article XIIIA; Article XXVIII
Contracts
  wildlife habitat, 73, 74, 75
  Williamson Act, 13, 15, 21, 34–36, 73, 74
Costs
  with easements, 91–92, 93, 119
  with installment sales, 105
  with leases, 102, 111
Covenant, defined, 115. *See also* Restrictive covenants
Covenant not to sell, 107–108, 109
Cy pres doctrine, 112

Dakotas, 4
Date, on easement instrument, 93–94
Death tax credit, 72
Defeasible fee grants, 96–101
Deferred tax program, 12–13
Development, 2–3, 9–10, 59, 72, 77
  Conservation Easements Act and, 28, 33–34
  Open-Space Easement Act and, 24, 64, 65

Development (*continued*)
  Proposition 4 and, 12–13
  Williamson Act and, 15
Dingell, John, 48, 53, 54
Documentation of conservation
    values, easement instrument
    including, 82, 85–86
Drafting
  of conservation easement instru-
    ment, 81–94, 119
  of trust instruments, 112
Dunlap, John F., 17–18

Easements
  common law, 32–33, 113–114
  defined, 3–4, 113
  fishing, 5
  income tax deductions for, 19–20,
    21–22, 31, 36, 45–69, 71, 77, 84,
    86, 119
  vs. restrictive covenants/equitable
    servitudes, 117–118
  See also Conservation easements;
    Scenic easements
Easements in gross, 28, 46, 113, 114,
    115
Ecological importance. *See* Natural
    ecosystems
Economic Recovery Tax Act (ERTA),
    70
Educational purposes, 47, 50, 52–53
Eminent domain rights, 42, 43, 67
Enforceability
  of conservation easements, 29,
    30–31, 34, 49, 62, 64, 87, 111
  of defeasible fee grants, 96, 100
  with leases, 111
  of restrictive covenants/equitable
    servitudes, 117, 118
  subventions and, 39
Enforceable restrictions, 13, 15,
    36–37, 39, 61–62, 73–75, 76
Enforcement, of power of termina-
    tion, 98
Enforcement costs, 93, 119
Equitable servitudes, 28, 32, 115–118
Erosion, 2, 57

Estate tax, 45, 69–70, 71–73
Executory interests, 99, 153n189
Executory limitations, 63, 92,
    99–100, 101
Exhibits, in easement instrument, 94

Farmlands. *See* Agricultural lands
Federal government. *See* United
    States governmental entities
Federal taxes. *See under* Taxes
Fee gifts, 49, 61–62
Fee simple absolute, 95, 101–102
Fee simple determinable, 96, 97–98
Fee subject to a condition subse-
    quent, 96–98
Fee subject to an executory limita-
    tion, 96, 99
Finance Department, California,
    72–73
Fire control, 40
Fiscal constraints, government, 5, 69,
    91–92
Fish and Game Department, Cali-
    fornia, 44
Fish and Wildlife Service, United
    States, 4–5
Fishing easements, 5
Flexibility, in easement instrument,
    81
Flooding, 2, 57
Food supplies, 2
Forest land. *See* Timberland
Forest Taxation Reform Act, 38
Full-cash-value assessment method,
    74
Full fee techniques, 101–106

Gift taxes, 69–71
Governmental entities (general)
  and defeasible fee grants, 96
  fiscal constraints on, 5, 69, 91–92
  and full fee techniques, 101–102,
    103
  tax-deductible contributions to,
    49, 52, 55, 63, 64, 65, 67, 68, 103
  See also California state govern-
    mental entities; Local govern-

Governmental entities (general)
(*continued*)
mental entities; United States
governmental entities
Governmental immunity, from personal injury liability, 40–41
Government Code
Section 831, 40–41
Sections 6950–6954, 34. *See also*
Scenic Easement Deed Act
Sections 7301–7309, 71, 72–73,
151–152n161
Sections 16140–16154, 38
Section 35009, 10
Section 50280, 75
Sections 50575–50628, 40
Sections 51070–51097, 21–27, 37,
63, 66, 67, 68, 75–76, 123–131.
See also Open-Space Easement
Act of 1974
Sections 51100–51155, 38
Sections 51200–51295, 34–36. *See
also* Williamson Act
Section 65300, 23
Sections 65560–65570, 22–23, 37, 72
Section 65850, 37
Sections 65910–65912, 37
Government planning, 6, 23, 25, 28,
37, 57, 58
Grants, state, 39–40
Grazing lands, 88, 90
Great River Road, 4
Greenbelt statute, 10
Growth, 1, 2, 9–10, 12, 15. *See also*
Development

Habendum clause, in easement instrument, 93
Harman, John, 148n91
Health and safety, public, 23
Highway Beautification Act, 5
Highways, 4, 5, 16, 35, 42
Historical property, 4, 37, 47, 50, 53,
75, 147–148n86
Housing and Urban Development,
United States Department of, 5
Humboldt County, 6

Idaho, 4
Immunity, governmental, from injury liability, 40–41
Income capitalization method, 65,
73–74, 75, 78
Income tax deductions
for bargain sales, 103–104,
154n204
for defeasible fee gifts, 101
for easements, 19–20, 21–22, 31,
36, 45–69, 71, 77, 84, 86, 119
for installment sales, 105
with leases, 47, 110
for purchase and lease-back/sellback arrangements, 102, 103
of purchase options, 47, 108–109
for remainder interest, 46, 47,
61–62, 107
for restrictive covenants, 61, 118
for trusts, 63, 112, 113
for undivided interest in property,
46, 47, 54, 106
Williamson Act and, 36, 67
Inheritance tax, 71–73, 151–152n161
Injunctive relief, 29–30, 31, 117
Injury liability, 40–41, 111
Installment sale, 104–105
Integration, easement instrument
providing, 93
Intent, easement instrument stating,
85
Interest rates, 78
Internal Revenue Code (I.R.C.), 19,
105, 106, 108
Section 170, 46, 47, 48–69, 70, 71,
107, 108, 118
Section 212(3), 60
Section 501(c), 22, 30, 40, 63, 64
Section 1031(a), 104
Section 2032A, 70
Internal Revenue Service (IRS),
45–46, 103, 148n91. *See also* Internal Revenue Code

Jacobs, Andy, 48
Joint Committee on Open Space
Land, 14–15, 16, 37

Keene-Nejedly California Wetlands Preservation Act, 44

Land Conservation Act. *See* Williamson Act
Law codes. *See* Civil Code; Code of Civil Procedure; Government Code; Internal Revenue Code; Public Resources Code; Revenue and Taxation Code
Law Revision Commission, California, 98, 153n189
Leases, 47, 102, 110–111, 154–155n218
Life estate, 107
Local governmental entities (general)
  and Conservation Easements Act, 30, 31, 64, 75–76, 118
  and defeasible fee grants, 99
  easement instrument approved by, 94
  federal funding for, 5
  and Open-Space Easement Act, 17–27 passim, 36, 63, 66, 68, 94
  and Open Space Maintenance Act, 40
  planning by, 6, 23, 25, 37, 57, 58
  and Santa Monica Mountains Conservancy, 44
  and Scenic Easement Deed Act, 11–12, 34
  and State Coastal Conservancy, 44
  and Williamson Act, 13, 35, 36
Local land trusts, 5–6, 17, 18, 19, 27, 40–41, 63
Los Angeles County, 6, 144–145n32

Marin County, 6
Market value, 9–11, 12–14, 36, 65, 77
  abandonment fee and, 25
  in bargain sale, 103–104
  and estate tax, 70
  for income tax deductions, 59–60
  in purchase and lease-back arrangement, 102
  of purchase option, 108
Mendocino County, 6

Minerals, 49
Minnesota, 4, 5
Modification, easement, 32–34
Money damages, 31–32
Monterey County, 6, 11
Mount Vernon, 4

Napa County, 6
Natchez Trace Parkway, 4
National Park Service, 4, 44
Natural ecosystems, 1–2
  easements for, 4–5, 22, 23, 34, 50, 53–54, 88–89
  income tax deductions for, 47, 50, 53–54
  See also Wildlife habitats
Nature Conservancy, The, 27, 95, 143–144n10
Negative easements, 28–29, 113, 114, 115
New England, 5–6
New York, 5
Nonprofit conservation organizations, 5, 6–7, 101–102
  and bargain sale, 104
  and condemnation, 42, 67–68
  and Conservation Easements Act, 19, 20, 27–28, 30, 31, 63–64, 84, 101, 114, 118, 120
  and cost allocations, 92, 111
  and covenant not to sell, 107–108
  and defeasible fee grants, 96, 99–100, 101
  easement instrument identifying, 83–84
  and injury liability, 40–41, 111
  leases to, 110, 111
  and Open-Space Easement Act, 17–26 passim, 31, 63–64, 67–68, 84, 94, 101, 114, 120
  outright grants to, 95, 101–102
  and purchase options, 107–108
  and right of first refusal, 107–108
  and State Coastal Conservancy, 43, 44
  tax-deductible gifts to, 19–20,

Nonprofit conservation organizations (*continued*)
  21–22, 49–50, 52, 54, 61–68 passim, 84, 101–113 passim, 118
  tax exemptions for, 78–80
  trust gifts to, 112–113
  with undivided interest, 54, 106
  Williamson Act and, 36
Nonrenewal, notice of, 24, 74

Open space, defined, 34
Open space easement, in terminology, 8
Open-Space Easement Act of 1969, 16–17, 27, 34, 38, 73
Open-Space Easement Act of 1974, 9, 17–27, 31, 35–36, 114, 120
  and defeasible fee grants, 101
  easement instrument and, 84, 86, 87, 94
  and income tax deductions, 20, 21–22, 31, 36, 56, 58, 63–68, 70–71
  and property tax, 18–37 passim, 64–66, 73, 77
  and subventions, 27, 38
  text of, 123–131
  and zoning, 23, 37, 65, 67
Open Space Land Program, 5
Open Space Maintenance Act, 40
Open space use, defined, 22–23
Orange County, 6
Outright grant, 95, 101–102

Parks, 4, 5, 39, 43. *See also* Recreational land
Parks and Recreation Department, California, 5, 39–40, 44
Parties, easement instrument identifying, 83–84
Perpetuity
  defeasible fee grants in, 96
  of easements, 60–63, 66–67, 70–71, 86, 147–148n86
  leases for, 110

Personal injury liability, 40–41, 111
Pfeiffer–Big Sur State Park, 5
Pick-up tax, 71–72, 73
Planning, government, 6, 23, 25, 28, 37, 57, 58
Planning and Zoning Law, 22–23, 37
Point Lobos State Reserve, 5
Possibility of reverter, 97–98
Power of termination, 97–99, 101
Private conservation organizations.
  See Nonprofit conservation organizations
Private foundations, 52, 64
Privity of estate, 116
Property description, in easement instrument, 84
Property rights, 2–4, 19, 28, 43, 46
Property taxes, 9–40 passim, 45, 64–66, 73–80, 119
  with installment sale, 105
  with leases, 111
  Proposition 13 and, 19, 20, 26, 51, 65, 74, 76, 77–78
Proposition 3 (1966), 14, 36
Proposition 4 (1962), 12–13
Proposition 5 (1982), 71
Proposition 6 (1982), 71
Proposition 13 (1978), 51, 74, 76, 77–78
  and government fiscal constraints, 5
  and Open-Space Easement Act, 19, 20, 26, 65, 77
Public access, 22, 40–41, 53, 79, 87–88
Public health and safety, 23
Public interest/benefit, 22, 23–24, 50, 51–58, 84, 99
Public necessity, 42
Public Resources Code
  Sections 5500–5595, 39
  Sections 5620–5632, 39–40
  Sections 5780–5791, 39
  Sections 5810–5818, 44
  Sections 31000–31405, 42–44
  Sections 33000–33216, 42, 44

Public Works Board, California, 41, 43
Purchase and lease-back arrangement, 102–103
Purchase and sell-back arrangement, 103
Purchase option, 47, 107–109

Qualified conservation contribution, 48–49, 63–64

Recreational land, 4, 5, 10–11, 16, 23, 35–55 passim, 73, 79
Recreation and Park Districts Law, 39
Regional Park Districts Law, 39, 73
Relatively natural habitat, 53–54. *See also* Natural ecosystems
Remainder interest, 46, 47, 48, 61–62, 107
Renewal, easement, 24, 86
Rental value, 74, 102. *See also* Leases
Reservations, easement instrument specifying, 82, 86, 90–91
Resources Agency, California, 16, 37, 39, 72–73
Restrictions, 49
  in defeasible fee grants, 97
  easement instrument specifying, 81, 82, 83, 86, 88–90
  enforceable, 13, 15, 36–37, 39, 61–62, 73–75, 76
Restrictive covenants, 28, 32, 61, 109, 110, 115–118
Revenue and Taxation Code, 19
  Section 214, 78–79
  Section 402.1, 13, 76
  Section 402.5, 10–11, 12, 13
  Sections 421–430.5, 15, 18, 35, 36, 39, 73–75, 77
  Sections 431–437, 75
  Sections 439–439.4, 75
  Section 1630, 13
  Sections 13301–13304, 71–72
  Sections 13441–13443, 72
  Section 13841, 71, 72

  Section 13842, 71, 72
  Section 13957, 71, 72
  Section 17214, 71
  Section 24357, 71
Revenue Ruling 64-205, 45–46
Reversionary rights, 97–98
Reverter, 97–98
Right of first refusal, 107–108, 109
Right of reentry, 97
Right of way, 4
Rights
  with defeasible fee grant, 96
  easement, 82, 86, 87–88, 113–114
  eminent domain, 42, 43, 67
  property, 2–4, 19, 28, 43, 46
  reversionary, 97–98
Rivers, 4, 55, 69
Riverside County, 6
Roberti-Z'berg Urban Open Space and Recreation Program Act, 39–40
Rule against perpetuities, 99, 101, 109
Running covenants, 115–116

"Safe harbor" categories, 148n91
Salt ponds, 35
San Diego County, 6
San Francisco Bay, 55
San Mateo County, 6
Santa Barbara County, 6
Santa Catalina Island, 79, 144–145n32
Santa Catalina Island Conservancy v. *County of Los Angeles*, 79
Santa Clara County, 10
Santa Cruz County, 6
Santa Cruz Island, 143–144n10
Santa Monica Mountains Conservancy, 42, 44
Sawtooth National Recreation Area, 4
Scenic Easement Deed Act, 11–12, 14, 15, 20–21, 34
  easement instrument observing, 84
  Open-Space Easement Act and, 16, 20–21, 34

Scenic Easement Deed Act
(*continued*)
and Open Space Maintenance Act,
40
and property taxes, 12, 14, 34, 73
and purchase and lease-back arrangement, 103
and subventions, 38
Scenic easements, 4, 5, 11–12, 16, 23,
34
drafting of, 88, 89–90
income tax deductions for, 46, 50,
54–55, 57
and property tax, 12, 16, 34, 73
Scenic preservation (noneasement),
1, 35, 47
Senate Finance Committee Report,
50–61 passim, 69, 108, 118,
148n90
Severability, easement instrument
covering, 93
Shell, John, 151–152n161
Shoreline protection, 42–44, 57
Siedorf, Myron, 151–152n161
Sierra Club v. *City of Hayward*,
151n143
Signatures, on easement instrument,
93–94
Sonoma County, 6
State Coastal Commission, 43
State Coastal Conservancy, 31, 41,
42–44, 95, 103, 143–144n10
State Department of Finance, 72–73
State Department of Transportation,
42
State governments, federal funding
for, 5. *See also* California state
governmental entities
State Public Works Board, 41, 43
State Resources Agency, 16, 37, 39,
72–73
State taxes. *See under* Taxes
State Transportation Commission, 42
Subsequent deeds, easement instru-
ment covering, 92
Subventions, 27, 38–39

Suisun Marsh, 55
Supreme Court, California, 67, 79,
100
Sutton (Larry G.) v. *Commissioner*,
150n141

Tax benefit rule, 68
Tax deductions. *See* Income tax deductions
Taxes
California, 15–40 passim, 45, 51,
64–66, 71–80, 105, 119,
151–152n161. *See also* Income tax
deductions
capital gains, 71, 102, 103, 104,
estate, 45, 69–70, 71–73
inheritance, 71–73, 151–152n161
property, 9–40 passim, 45, 51,
64–66, 73–80, 105, 119
United States, 6–7, 22, 30, 40,
69–71, 102–105 passim, 148n91.
See also Income tax deductions
Tax exemption, welfare, 78–80
Tax Reduction and Simplification
Act, 47
Tax Reform Act, 46, 47
Tax Treatment Extension Act, 48, 51,
132–134
Tenants-in-common, 106
Termination
of defeasible fee grants, 97–99
easement, 32–34, 68, 114
Terms (temporal)
of easements, 17, 24, 27, 66, 67,
70–71, 86, 147–148n86
of leases, 110
of trusts, 111
of Williamson Act contracts, 35
See also Perpetuity
Timberland
defined, 38
easements involving, 57–58, 70,
74, 88, 90
estate tax and, 70
income tax deduction and, 57–58
property tax and, 38, 74, 75

Timberland (*continued*)
  zoned, 38, 75
Timberland Productivity Act, California, 38
Transferability
  of development rights, 3
  of easements, 26, 29, 113
Transfer in trust, 111–113
Transportation Department, California, 42
Treasury Department, United States, 46–60 passim, 67–68, 69, 148–149n97
Trust for Public Land, The, 6, 27, 95
Trusts
  local land, 5–6, 17, 18, 19, 27, 40–41, 63
  transferring in, 111–113

Undivided interest in property, 46, 47, 54, 105–106
United States Department of Housing and Urban Development, 5
United States Fish and Wildlife Service, 4–5
United States governmental entities (general)
  and California conservation easement law, 31, 114
  easements held by, 4–5, 30, 114
  state and local funding by, 5
  wildlife habitat contracts with, 73
United States law codes. *See* Internal Revenue Code
United States National Park Service, 4, 44
United States taxes. *See under* Taxes
United States Treasury Department, 46–60 passim, 67–68, 69, 148–149n97
Urban property leases, 110
Uses, land, 2
  easement draft specifying, 86, 90–91
  open space, 22–23
Use valuation
  for estate taxes, 70
  for property taxes, 9–40 passim, 73–80

Valuation
  for estate taxes, 70
  for income tax deductions, 58–60
  for property taxes, 9–40 passim, 73–80
  See also Market value
Vested interest, 99, 109

Waterfowl breeding habitats, 4–5
Water quality, 57
Watersheds, 23, 38
Water supplies, 2, 57
Welfare tax exemption, 78–80
Wetlands, 4–5, 35, 44
Wild and Scenic Rivers Act, 69
Wildlife habitats
  California Timberland Productivity Act and, 38
  under contracts (non-Williamson Act), 73, 74, 75
  easements for, 4–5, 23
  income tax deductions for, 53
  Williamson Act and, 35
Williamson Act, 13–21 passim, 34–36, 37, 38, 67–77 passim, 151n143
Wisconsin, 4, 5

Z'berg-Warren-Keene-Collier Forest Taxation Reform Act, 38
Zoning, 2, 10–11, 37
  and income tax deduction, 59, 65, 67
  and Open-Space Easement Act, 23, 37, 65, 67
  timberland, 38, 75

The Conservation Easement in California is the latest volume in a series of books published by Island Press that make available state-of-the-art information on all aspects of conservation and land use to professionals and laypeople at work in these fields. Other titles in this series as well as titles of related interest are available directly from Island Press, Star Route 1, Box 38, Covelo, California 95428.

Private Options: Tools and Concepts for Land Conservation, by Montana Land Reliance and Land Trust Exchange. $25.00

This volume presents practical methods of preserving land, based on the experience of more than thirty experts. Topics include income tax incentives for preserving agricultural land, marketing land conservation, management of conserved land areas, and the real estate business as a conservation tool.

Building an Ark: Tools for the Preservation of Natural Diversity Through Land Protection, by Phillip M. Hoose. Illustrations. $12.00

The author is national protection planner for The Nature Conservancy, and this book presents a comprehensive plan that can be used to identify and protect what remains of each state's natural ecological diversity. Case studies augment this blueprint for conservation.

Tree Talk: The People and Politics of Timber, by Ray Raphael. Illustrations by Mark Livingston. $12.00

A probing analysis of modern forestry practices and philosophies. In a balanced and informed text, *Tree Talk* presents the views of loggers, environmentalists, timber industry executives, and forest farmers and goes beyond the politics of "production versus protection" to propose new ways to harvest trees and preserve forest habitats in a healthy economy and a thriving environment.

Pocket Flora of the Redwood Forest, by Dr. Rudolf W. Becking. Illustrations. $15.00

The most useful and comprehensive guidebook available for the plants of the world-famous redwood forest. Dr. Rudolf W. Becking, a noted botanist and Professor of Natural Resources, is also a gifted artist. The *Pocket Flora* includes detailed drawings, a complete key, and simple, accurate descriptions for 212 of the most common species of this unique plant community, as well as eight pages of color photographs. Plasticized cover for field use.

A Citizen's Guide to Timber Harvest Plans, by Marylee Bytheriver. Illustrations. $1.50

California state law permits any interested citizen to learn the details of proposed timber cutting on private or public lands. This report instructs citizens on their rights concerning timber harvesting, the procedures for influencing the details of proposed logging operations, and the specialized vocabulary surrounding the Timber Harvest Plan. A resource for action.

An Everyday History of Somewhere, by Ray Raphael. Illustrations by Mark Livingston. $8.00

This work of history and documentation embraces the life and work of ordinary people, from the Indians who inhabited the coastal forests of northern California to the loggers, tanbark strippers, and farmers who came after them. This loving look at history takes us in a full circle that leads to the everyday life of us all.

Two Californias: The Truth About the Split-State Movement, by Michael DiLeo and Eleanor Smith. $10.95

A timely and provocative examination of the issues that underlie the split-state movement in California, with special focus on the question of resources. A book that is likely to change the ways we think about living together and sharing resources in the 1980s.

The Trail North, by Hawk Greenway. Illustrations. $7.50

The summer adventure of a young man who traveled the spine of coastal mountains from California to Washington with only his horse for a companion. The book he has made from this journey reveals his coming of age as he studies, reflects, and greets the world that is awakening within and around him.

America Without Violence: Why Violence Persists and How You Can Stop It, by Michael N. Nagler. Foreword by Louis Jolyon West, M.D. $8.00

Challenging the widespread assumption that violence is an inevitable part of human existence, *America Without Violence* asserts that it *is* possible to live in a nonviolent society. The choice, Michael Nagler says, begins with each individual. In personal, practical language, *America Without Violence* explains how to make the changes in our private lives that can counteract the forces of violence throughout our society.

The Book of the Vision Quest: Personal Transformation in the Wilderness, by Steven Foster with Meredith E. Little. Photographs. $10.00

The inspiring record of modern people enacting an ancient, archetypal rite of passage. This book shares the wisdom and the seeking of many persons who have known the opportunity to face themselves, their fears, and their courage, and to live in harmony with nature through the experience of the traditional Vision Quest. Excerpts from participants' journals add an intimate dimension to this unique account of human challenge.

Wellspring: A Story from the Deep Country, by Barbara Dean. Illustrations. $6.00

The moving, first-person account of a contemporary woman's life at the edge of wilderness. Since 1971, Barbara Dean has lived in a handmade yurt on land she shares with fifteen friends. Their struggles, both hilarious and poignant, form the background for this inspiring story of personal growth and deep love for nature.

Headwaters: Tales of the Wilderness, by Ash, Russell, Doog, and Del Rio. Preface by Edward Abbey. Photographs and illustrations. $6.00

Four bridge-playing buddies tackle the wilderness—they go in separately, meet on top of a rock, and come out talking. These four are as different as the suits in their deck of cards, as ragged as a three-day beard, and as eager as sparks.

No Substitute for Madness: A Teacher, His Kids & The Lessons of Real Life, by Ron Jones. Illustrations. $8.00

Seven magnificent glimpses of life as it is. Ron Jones is a teacher with the gift of translating human beauty into words and knowing where to find it in the first place. This collection of true experiences includes "The Acorn People," the moving story of a summer camp for handicapped kids, and "The Third Wave," a harrowing experiment in Nazi training in a high school class—both of which were adapted for television movies.

Perfection Perception, with the Brothers O. and Joe de Vivre. $5.00

Notes from a metaphysical journey through the mountains of Patagonia. The authors share their experiences and discoveries in using their powers of perception to change the world. Their thoughts are mystical at times, but their basis is firmly experiential and parallels the most theoretically advanced works in modern physics.

The Search for Goodbye-to-Rains, by Paul McHugh. $7.50

Steve Gertane takes to the road in an American odyssey that is part fantasy and part real—a haphazard pursuit that includes Faulkner's Mississippi, the rarefied New Mexico air, and a motorcycle named Frank. "A rich, resonant novel of the interior world. Overtones of Whitman, Kerouac."—Robert Anton Wilson

---

Please enclose $1.00 with each order for postage and handling.
California residents, add 6% sales tax.
A catalog of current and forthcoming titles is available free of charge.